Sporting Slip-Ups
and
Goalmouth Gaffes

Sporting Slip-Ups and Goalmouth Gaffes

Breathtaking Blunders from the World of Sport

Stephen Blake and Andrew John

First published in Great Britain in 2002 by
Michael O'Mara Books Limited
9 Lion Yard
Tremadoc Road
London SW4 7NQ

A CIP catalogue record for this book is available from the British Library

ISBN 1-85479-858-8

1 3 5 7 9 10 8 6 4 2

Designed and typeset by Design 23

Printed and bound in Finland by WS Bookwell, Juva

Contents

Introduction
6

On Track and Field
7

Your Ringside Seat
28

The Leather and the Willow
43

On Fairway and Green
68

Thrills On Wheels
80

The Sport of Kings
91

Blood, Mud and Machismo
104

Putting the Boot In
119

Oddballs
144

**Out of the Mouths of Sportsmen
and Commentators...**
159

Introduction

Sport should be fun, even when it's being taken deadly seriously. In fact, that's when it's the most fun, because it's when the deadly serious get their comeuppance or their pride bubble is burst that we tend to laugh the most. We've all had that sense of *schadenfreude* when a sportsman who's been doing so well throws it all away on the last hole, or the last penalty shot, or the last ball, or the last furlong, or the last lap.

Not all the stories in our collection feature such mishaps, but there are plenty that do. Some reveal plain stupidity, some bad luck. Some are funny, others just interesting in a quirky sort of way. *Sporting Slip-Ups and Goalmouth Gaffes* takes a light-hearted look at things that have gone wrong in the world of sport; a collection of events that might otherwise be forgotten.

We have found stories in a variety of ways – trawling through books and records, surfing the Internet, talking to sporting friends, reading newspapers and magazines – and have enjoyed bringing to you some of the wackier moments of sport, such as when the autograph-signing famous golfer found himself pushed into the lake by adoring fans; when the US president's golf ball hit a woman spectator between the eyes, shattering her glasses; when a famous racing driver pulled down an awning on to his boss's head because he had forgotten to unhook the air line as he set off for the starting grid, and the story of the football team that ended the season with minus one point.

Our collection of stories spans three centuries, featuring some celebrated tales, and some not so well known, from the nineteenth century through to the present day. We hope you will find them as entertaining and amusing as we do.

Stephen Blake and Andrew John
April 2002

On Track and Field

There is nothing like the Olympic or Commonwealth Games to rouse our national spirit. Whether in track or field events, we are all rooting for 'our' woman and man out there, jumping, sprinting, flinging a javelin or putting a shot.

Here is our own 'running' commentary on some of the wackier moments in the history of athletics.

And the winner is ... the loser

The men's 400-yards final at the 1938 Empire Games in Sydney was such a close race that it caused an unprecedented toing and froing of the coveted prize.

After a fifteen-minute wait, England's Bill Roberts and Canadian Bill Fritz finally heard the officials' verdict. Initially they declared that Roberts had crossed the line first. But after another discussion it was announced that another decision had been reached – Fritz was the winner.

Canadians were celebrating, but not for long. Officials gathered once more and mumbled among themselves. They then announced the winner for the final time – it was Roberts again!

Dogged determination

At the 1950 Empire Games in Auckland, New Zealand, forty-three-year-old Jack Holden of England won the marathon, despite having had to remove his running shoes, which were soaked by a sudden downpour, and complete the course barefoot.

What made his win even more surprising, however, was the distracting presence of a pesky dog that insisted on following him, in spite of his polite attempts to tell the irksome canine where to go. At one point the dog nearly tripped him up, until race officials managed to guide it away.

Everyone's a winner, baby

Australia's Gary Holdsworth was asked to hand over the bronze medal he had won – or thought he had won – for the men's 100-yards race in the 1962 Commonwealth Games in Perth. Some days after the event, an appeals jury looked at a print of the finish and decided that the third place was gained not by Holdsworth but by his team-mate, Mike Cleary.

Holdsworth was quoted as shouting at officials, 'You've got to be joking, haven't you? My time was listed faster.'

Oddly enough, photographic evidence had not been called for on the day, but a photograph had been taken, and it was this that led the appeals jury to make their final decision. It showed that Cleary was 5 centimetres (2 inches) ahead of his fellow Australian. As a compromise, however, both men were awarded a bronze medal.

Going with the wind

In 1960, at the West German Athletics Championships, Manfred Steinbach would have been just a centimetre short of Jesse Owens's world-record, 8.15-metre long jump, which had stood since 1935.

Steinbach's fourth leap measured 8.14 metres, but the official in charge, Walter Blume, announced that the following wind was 3.2 metres per second. That was 1.2 metres per second higher than the permissible level of 2.0, and so the distance was not recorded.

Blume later admitted, however, that he had not had a wind gauge working for that particular jump, and rather than admit to such a major professional oversight, he gave a wind speed that would have rendered the record invalid. Adding to Steinbach's frustration, it emerged that the wind on all his other jumps that day was not above 1.1 metres per second.

It's a lock-out

During the 1979 Pan American Games in San Juan in Puerto Rico, Wallace Williams of the Virgin Islands was trailing by about thirty-nine minutes when the runner in front of him had entered the stadium.

Poor Wallace got to the stadium and found it locked. Everybody had gone home.

Rarin' to go

Exhibiting the highest level of hearty sporting enthusiasm, a supremely keen pack of runners in the Boston marathon in 1900 produced an extraordinary false start.

There were a large number of Canadian runners in the field

who were so full of adrenaline and ready to race that, as soon as the starter, John Graham, had finished his official speech, but before he could officially start the race, off they sprinted.

Keep your eye on that one, Boyd

Excuses, excuses! Probably the most original one came from the American 400-metre hurdler Boyd Gittins, who was taking part in the 1968 Olympic trials in the United States.

Gittins's reason for being eliminated was that a pigeon dropping had hit him in the eye and one of his contact lenses had been dislodged just as he was about to take the first hurdle.

Lap of dishonour (1)

Sometimes it is possible to achieve gold in spite of a sporting slip-up, as New Zealand's Billy Savidan discovered.

The occasion was the 1930 Empire Games at Hamilton in Canada, and a track official made a blunder by turning over one card too many on the counter that tells runners how many laps are remaining.

Savidan thought he was on the last lap, but he was not. After he had sprinted down the home straight, he was told he still had a lap to run. He had stopped running at this point and seemed not to believe what he was being told.

Once the awful truth was confirmed for him, he had no option but to carry on, and with an amazing last-ditch effort, he managed to complete the final lap – the real final lap – and win gold, with England's Ernest Harper in hot pursuit. He collapsed in the dressing room before he received his medal.

Then, after all the fuss surrounding the event, the band played the English anthem, 'Land of Hope and Glory', instead of the New Zealand anthem.

Lap of dishonour (2)

During a competition between Africa and the United States in 1971, the Ethiopian runner Miruts Yifter thought he was on the last lap and had all but used his last ounce of energy to cross the finishing line, only to discover that it was just the penultimate lap. Having thoroughly exhausted himself, all Yifter could do was jog around the last lap, leaving it to Steve Prefontaine of the United States to run past him and win the race.

Success went to his head

James Trapp, from Clemson University in the United States, had a dizzying moment after coming third in a 200-metres college event, when he was bashed over the head with the trophy.

The winner of the race, Dave Braunskill, had lifted the trophy aloft in triumph following his victory, but Trapp's head got in the way and needed several stitches.

Majestic throw

Whether royalist or republican, it is simply not acceptable to go around throwing hammers at royalty, unless one wishes to spend the rest of one's days languishing in the Tower.

Queen Elizabeth II must have been in a good mood at the 1978 Commonwealth Games at Edmonton, therefore, when a hammer came hurtling above the heads of photographers and landed not far from her, narrowly missing a CBS cameraman during its wayward journey. Officials decided that the hammer competition would be better postponed until after the royal party had left the stadium.

The Games were next held in Canada in 1994. When organizers were asked on which day they would prefer to hold the hammer event, they replied, 'Any day the Queen isn't there.'

The dizziness of the long-distance runner

A sense of direction is rather important to a runner. It helps to be able to find one's way to the finish line, after all.

However, during the marathon in the 1954 European Championships in Berne, Ivan Filin of Russia had just overtaken Finland's Veikko Karvonen, and stormed into the stadium, certain to win.

But then he went that way and ran for more than a hundred metres before he realized he should have gone this way. Or was it the other way? Whichever way, he came third.

Milk of unkindness

When Samuel Ferris of Great Britain was out on a training run to familiarize himself with the course of the 1932 Olympic marathon in Los Angeles, he decided he would use a huge milk advertisement as a marker for his final effort, about a mile (1.5km) from the finish.

On race day, however, he did not see his marker. In front of the advertisement a grandstand had been erected, so poor old Ferris could not see it. He did not win either, and he got the silver instead of the gold he had expected to achieve. He was a full minute behind the winner Juan Carlos Zabala of Argentine, when he entered the stadium.

Not for the high jump

In the 1912 Olympic high jump in Stockholm, Germany's Hans Liesche had to jump 6 feet 4 inches (1.9 metres) to equal the best effort of the United States' Alma Richards.

Having already had two failures at the height, Liesche was entitled to only one more attempt. With great concentration, he composed himself and prepared for his moment, but was thwarted by the loud bang of a gun, signalling the start of a track race.

Liesche had to wait for the race to end before he could prepare himself mentally to try again. The moment he had regained his composure, the stadium band began to play and Liesche's nerves were in tatters.

Knowing he could not hold back for much longer (indeed, a Swedish official had already told him to hurry), he completed his run and jump half-heartedly, resulting in a dismal failure for the unfortunate German.

Pardon my French

Loren Murchison of the United States was in confusion at the beginning of the 1920 Olympic men's 100-metres final because of a translation problem.

The Games were being held in Antwerp, Belgium, and the starter was speaking French, When he said 'prêt', Murchison thought the competitors had been told to stand up, though literally the word means 'ready', that is 'get set' within the context of a race.

However, Murchison was relaxing his body and getting to his feet when 'Bang!' – off went the starting pistol. The American trailed his fellow competitors by 9 metres (10 yards), and came last.

Pot luck

It was the occasion of the 4,000-metres cross-country, the final event of the modern pentathlon during the 1984 Olympic Games in Los Angeles, and Svante Rasmuson of Sweden had pulled clear. However, just 18 metres (20 yards) from the finish, he fell over a potted plant, put there to brighten up the course. Unfortunately for Rasmuson, it did not brighten his day. Before he could get back on his feet, Italy's Daniele Masala shot past him and won gold.

The heat was off for Wym

It turned out to be a wasted journey for Wym Essajas of Surinam (formerly Dutch Guiana, in South America) when he became the first person to be chosen to represent his country in the 1960 Olympic Games in Rome.

He was due to take part in the men's 800-metre race, but a breakdown in communications had ruined his chances. Wym had been told that the heats were taking place in the afternoon, but in actual fact they were scheduled for the morning.

Naturally, he had spent the morning resting and mentally preparing for the heats, only to find that, on arrival at the stadium, they had already taken place.

So he returned to Surinam, having missed the opportunity to make Olympic Games history for his country.

Road runners

During the Sixteenth World Student Games in Sheffield in 1991, three Mozambican athletes decided to go on a training run. So they found a nice long smooth road, all made of good-quality tarmac, which was perfect for their needs. What they failed to realize was that they were running along the hard shoulder of the M1.

Police soon got them back on track, by escorting them to a local sports ground where they could continue their practice.

We have ignition – but then again ...

Sheffield-born Helen Sharman was Britain's first astronaut and, when athletics organizers needed a celebrity to take part in the opening ceremony of the Sixteenth World Student Games, Sharman was the natural choice.

Perhaps she was still feeling the effects of weightlessness after her travels in space, for Sharman, who was to perform the symbolic job of lighting the flame to declare the Games open, managed to trip on a red carpet in the stadium, and dropped the flaming torch, extinguishing it completely.

Have no gun, cannot travel
There was a hold-up at the start of the Jamaican national track championships in 1966 because no one had remembered to bring the starting pistol. Perhaps someone should have just shouted 'Bang!'

Silver bubbles
There were just two miles to go for Charles Hefferon of South Africa in the 1908 London Olympic marathon, when he made the fateful decision to accept a drink of champagne.

The bubbly did not give him the fizz required to strike gold; on the contrary, it made him disoriented and eventually gave him stomach cramps.

But he did manage to win a silver medal.

That's our race!
It must have been quite disconcerting to be watching television only to see athletes lining up to begin the race in which you were supposed to be taking part.

It happened during the 1972 Munich Olympics, when two American runners, Eddie Hart and Rey Robinson, were among the favourites to win the men's 100-metres race.

Frustratingly, the athletes never arrived, thanks to their coach who had misread the starting time.

So, as they watched television while waiting for the team bus at the Olympic village, Robinson was horrified to see athletes lining up for the race that he had expected to win.

What a splashing fellow!

While Sergei Skrypka of the Soviet Union was competing in a heat of the 3,000-metres steeplechase in the 1972 Olympic Games in Munich, he managed to lose one of his shoes.

There were six laps to go and, despite his half-shod status, Skrypka managed to keep up with the leaders.

But on the final water jump, Sergei's bare foot slipped on the wet barrier, and sent him plummeting headlong into the water.

The victorious loser

For the 1908 Olympic marathon in London, a decision was made to add a few more yards to the distance so that the runners could finish in front of the royal box – a total of 385 yards (352 metres) in fact.

The extra yardage proved to be just too much for the race leader, Italy's Dorando Pietri, who began to falter on the downward ramp that led to the cinder track. He was directed to the left instead of to the right as he had expected, and in his confusion he stumbled – 385 yards from the finish.

Although his legs were like jelly, he managed to get to his feet, and fell four times as he stumbled towards the line, where his last fall occurred, just short of the finish. The chief race organizer, Jack Andrew, went to help Pietri across the line and the athlete was taken away on a stretcher.

But matters did not end there. US runner John Hayes came in second, about half a minute after Pietri had been helped across the line, and while the Italian team were celebrating their victory, the Americans protested that the result was unfair, and Pietri was duly disqualified.

The mustachioed Italian was back to normal the following day, and said the official should not have helped him, because he was sure he could have finished the race under his own steam. Jack Andrew, now feeling rather awkward about the whole thing, then maintained that he had not actually helped the runner, but merely caught him as he fell at the tape.

Though Pietri was denied his day of victory officially, many thought the situation so unfair that he was later presented with an inscribed gold cup as compensation. Furthermore he was fêted back in Italy, the subject of many songs and poems.

Ushered in at last
When politics get in the way of the chance of Olympic stardom, life can be frustrating.

Consider the misfortune of the Rhodesian javelin thrower Bruce Kennedy who, in 1972, was selected for his national team for the Munich Olympics. There was a ban on Rhodesian participation, however, so Kennedy was denied the chance to compete.

Four years later in Montreal, he was again chosen, but Rhodesia – which had not yet become Zimbabwe – was still not allowed to take part.

Bruce decided to apply for US citizenship in 1977, and managed to make it to the 1980 Moscow Olympics as part of the American team but, owing to the Soviet invasion of Afghanistan, the US opted to boycott the Games.

Kennedy finally got to the Los Angeles Games in 1984, working as a stadium usher.

Wheels of misfortune

Entering a marathon as an able-bodied wheelchair athlete is not to be encouraged. Daniel Sadler committed this very act in 2002, which led to his being banned from the London Marathon, despite the fact that he had been racing in wheelchairs for twelve years.

Kevin Baker of the British Wheelchair Sports Foundation, told the *Sun* that his organization backed the ban. 'It may just be Dan now,' he told the tabloid, 'but if he was allowed to compete, what would stop someone going into any secondary school and training a group of students to be wheelchair racing stars? In a decade disabled people would feel at a disadvantage. They'd find they'd lost one of their few sports.'

Twenty-four-year-old Sadler, from Chessington in Surrey, began racing in wheelchairs because his father, who was paralysed from the waist down, was a competitor.

Sadler Jr finished third in the 2001 Great North Run, dressed in a Paralympics kit. He won a £200 prize, but it was taken back by organizers when they realized he was able-bodied. The International Paralympic Committee has banned Mr Sadler from its races.

However, he was not without support. Tanni Grey-Thompson, winner of four wheelchair gold medals at the Sydney Paralympics said, 'People assume Dan has an unfair advantage. He hasn't. He may have stomach muscles that work, but he's carrying more weight, he gets leg cramps, and he makes a less aerodynamic shape.'

Far-flung

Records were not the only things broken at an athletics event held in north-east England in 1952.

The hammer thrower twirled his hammer around, let go, and off it went, landing outside the enclosure, right on the bonnet of his own Triumph Spitfire, which he had arranged to sell that night. He had to spend £150 to fix the damage.

The hammer's journey had only just begun, for after bouncing off the bonnet of the car, it went straight through the window of the stadium office, knocking unconscious an official.

It was not the first time that the hammer thrower had caused such havoc; previously he had hit a petrol station, a gents' toilet – from which a spectator emerged hurriedly, thinking it had been struck by lightning – and a police car.

Taking the Flack

Australia's Edwin Flack was exhausted by the time he was nearly 5 km (3 miles) from the finishing line during the 1896 Olympic marathon in Athens.

So tired was he that he seemed likely to collapse into an ungainly heap, until someone asked a Greek spectator to help him. In his delirious state, however, Flack thought the spectator was about to attack him, and he punched the helpful chap to the ground.

Flack decided to retire from the race after that.

White lies?

An unusual story appeared in the BBC's Sport Online website about how the singer Barry White had indirectly helped an athlete to fail a drugs test.

When a urine sample taken from the 1992 Olympic 100-metre bronze medallist Dennis Mitchell failed a drugs test, the athlete affirmed that the testosterone in his body was nothing to do with having taken a banned substance. In fact his reason was a little more embarrassing than that; the night before the test, Mitchell had been at home with his wife listening to Barry White on the stereo and, while drinking five bottles of beer, the sprinter said he made love to his wife four times.

He received a two-year ban for his night of passion, and it is said he introduced a rota system at home, to avoid making the same mistake again.

Traffic hold-up

In the 1984 Olympic women's marathon in Los Angeles, Honduran athlete Leda Diaz de Cano had become separated from the rest of the runners. In fact she was so far behind the other competitors – a total of 27 minutes, 20 km (12.4 miles) – that officials had to persuade her to retire so they could reopen the streets to traffic.

You've got to hand it to him

When a former British discus champion, Gerry Carr, took part in a special 'heavyweights' relay race for University College in Los Angeles, in 1962, it seems he did not know his own strength. Competing against runners from Stanford University, he grabbed the baton hard, and it promptly broke.

Unseen, unsung

The stupidity of the American officials at the 1932 Olympic Games in Los Angeles is very hard to beat. John Anderson of the United States was leading the men's discus competition, and when Jules Noël of France launched his fourth throw, it appeared to land ahead of Anderson's leading distance.

Unfortunately, the officials were all watching a pole vault close by, and did not see where Noël's throw had landed.

Offered another throw as compensation, Noël was unable to repeat the disputed performance, and missed out on a crucial opportunity to challenge for top spot.

Not-so-fast Fast

There were just 6.5 km (about 4 miles) to go in the 1900 Olympic marathon in Paris, and Ernst Fast, a nineteen-year-old Swede, was in the lead. For some reason, however, he and the cyclist accompanying him took a wrong turning along the marathon route.

After discovering his error it was too late to recover the lost time and he had to settle for third place.

Right on the button

During the 1950 Empire Games, spectators were baffled by the behaviour of the South African hurdler Tom Avery who, during the final of the 120-yard hurdles event, was holding up his shorts by the waist.

It transpired that a button had come loose and fallen from his shorts as soon as he started to run. If he had not held them up, not only would he have caused himself a touch of embarrassment, but he would also have tripped up and landed on his face.

Despite his unfortunate handicap, he won bronze.

And the band played on

At the Helsinki Olympics in 1952 no one had expected Luxembourg to win gold, and so no one had given the band the score for the country's national anthem.

Luxembourg did win gold, however, through their runner Josef Barthel.

At the medal ceremony, the band had to improvise, and nobody noticed the difference.

Dogged by bad luck (1)

The African runner Lentauw thought he was going to make a great finish in the 1904 Olympic marathon at St Louis, but despite his efforts he could finish only ninth.

His progress had been severely hampered while being chased off the course and through a cornfield by two large dogs.

Dogged by bad luck (2)

A dog is not always a man's best friend – especially when that man is trying to win a marathon.

The events of 1961 proved this to be the case when John J. Kelley of the United States was almost level with Eino Oksanen of Finland during the 1961 Boston marathon. As the two men battled it out, a stray dog decided to join in, unaware of how important the race was for his two-legged fellow runners, who had to keep breaking stride as the dog kept impeding their progress.

Eventually, 27 km (17 miles) into the race, Kelley fell over the clumsy canine and needed to be helped to his feet by another runner. The incident cost him valuable time and ultimately the race, because he finished second – just twenty-five seconds behind the Finn.

Wottle he do now?

After US Olympic, 800-metre gold-medal winner Dave Wottle forgot to remove his cap when 'The Star-Spangled Banner' was being played at the medal ceremony in Munich in 1972, he reacted as though he had committed an appalling and unforgivable crime.

Overcome with emotion, distraught and tearful, Wottle made a humble and formal apology to the American people for offending his nation's pride.

Yifter's eight-year wait

If you want to get ahead, avoid getting stuck in the loo. It happened to the Ethiopian distance runner Miruts Yifter ('Yifter the Shifter', as he was better known) in the 1972 Munich Olympics. He missed the start of a 5,000-metres heat because he was in the toilet, and could not reach the track in time.

Ethiopia boycotted the 1976 Olympics so Yifter had to wait eight years to have another attempt at winning the 5,000-metres gold. In 1980 he eventually claimed his crown.

Country style

During the Olympic cross-country event in 1924, which was run over a distance of 10,000 metres (6.21 miles), the competitors began dropping like flies.

Not only was it a very hot day in Paris, but some of the runners were overcome by noxious fumes coming from a nearby energy plant. If that were not enough, parts of the circuit were covered with knee-high thistles.

There were mishaps, too. When Aguilar of Spain entered the stadium he hit his head on a marker. Sewell of Great Britain had headed off in the wrong direction and had to be told which way to run. Having been thus redirected, he banged into a fellow runner. Both men fell and did not finish the course. Paavo Nurmi of Finland got the gold.

A walk on the wildly expensive side

It was an expensive way to win the 50-km walk, but Don Thompson of Great Britain decided that to be fully prepared, he needed to acclimatize himself. It would be hot in Rome in the 1960 Olympic Games, and so Don converted his bathroom into a sauna by turning up the gas to its highest level.

During the eighteen months before the Games he sat, or probably marked time, in his bathroom to get used to the sweltering heat and, in the process, notched up a gas bill of £9,763.

When he returned from his Olympic triumph, he discovered the gas board had cut him off.

Winner's loss

The Russian athlete Ivanon Vyacheslav was thrilled to win a medal at the 1956 Melbourne Olympics. He was so thrilled, in fact, that in his excitement he threw the medal high into the air.

It landed in Lake Wendouree, and was never found.

Clang!

When you drop a clanger, it is advisable not to do it front of millions of spectators, both in the stadium and across the world glued to television sets, but it happened at the start of the final lap of a 5,000-metres heat during the 1978 Commonwealth Games.

The official tolled the bell to signal the final lap, and the bell responded by falling off its stand in a most undignified manner.

Do share my lunch

France's Joseph Guillemot was not feeling too well. During the 1920 Olympic Games in Antwerp, the king of Belgium had requested that the 10,000-metres race be brought forward from 5.30 p.m. to 2.15 p.m.

Unfortunately Guillemot had not been informed of the change in timing, and had just eaten a hearty lunch. So, when Paavo Nurmi of Finland won the race, Guillemot – who was the runner-up – was sick all over him.

Ripe for failure

A Cuban postman named Feliz Carvajal was taking part in the 1904 Olympic marathon, but was denied a medal after a spot of tummy trouble.

It was his own fault, however, as he had stopped to talk to some spectators en route, and had eaten some unripe fruit. The resulting indigestion relegated him to fourth place.

Fast track to frustration (1)

'I laughed, but I felt like crying,' said South Africa's Johannes Coleman after being told his new world record could not be ratified. 'It must have been my fastest ever marathon.'

The occasion was the 1938 Natal marathon at Alexander Park, Pietermaritzburg. The world record at the time stood at 2 hours, 26 minutes and 42 seconds. As he entered the park at the end of his run, Coleman's own watch indicated that he had completed the race in 2 hours and 23 minutes.

He went in search of Harold Sulin, the chief timekeeper, to confirm his score, but found him with colleagues drinking tea in the refreshment room. They were most apologetic, admitting that no one had expected Coleman or any of the runners to finish the race so quickly. So the record could not be ratified.

Fast track to frustration (2)

Runners were told to go the wrong way when they entered the stadium at the end of the 1912 Polytechnic Harriers marathon in London. Instead of the 840 yards they would have run, they only completed 480 yards.

Unfortunately for James Corkery of Canada, who thought he had achieved a world record, he was told his time could not be recognized because it was short of the full marathon distance.

A celebrated defeat

Alex Wilson of Canada was sure he had achieved victory in the men's 800-metres final during the 1932 Olympic Games in Los Angeles. So sure, in fact, that he threw up his arms while still a yard from the finish. His celebratory gesture proved to be premature, however, for as he eased his speed a little, while his hands were in the air, Britain's Tommy Hampson put on a final – and, for Wilson, fatal – spurt, and went past him. Wilson was fated never to win Olympic gold.

Beware of Greeks blowing trumpets

The United States team thought they had got everything nicely planned when they set off for the 1896 Olympics in Athens (the last time they were held there, incidentally, before 2004). They spent between sixteen and seventeen days at sea, and thought, when they arrived in Athens on 5 April, that they had another twelve days before the Games began.

However, they had not realized that Greece was still using the Julian calendar, and was eleven days ahead; and so the Americans got a nasty surprise when, after the end of their long journey, they awoke to the sound of a brass band proclaiming the commencement of the Games.

Contraflow on legs

Confusion reigned at the end of the 1946 Amateur Athletic Association marathon at the White City stadium in London when Squire Yarrow and Donald McNab Robertson stormed on to the track.

A steeplechase was still in progress, and so the marathon runners had to dodge hurdles, not to mention other runners.

They managed it however, and Yarrow got there just ahead of Robertson.

Your Ringside Seat

With its charmless machismo, it could be thought that an activity such as boxing, in which the object is to batter one's opponent into submission, would be the last sport to bring forth amusement and mirth. This has proved not to be the case, however, as the following pages contain a number of knockout stories, guaranteed to raise a smile.

Caught napping

The occasion of the world middleweight title fight between Billy Papke and the challenger, George Bernard of France, in Paris in December 1912, produced one of the more unusual endings to a fight in boxing history. There was no knockout or a win on points. In fact, it was all rather anti-climactic.

Between the sixth and seventh rounds Bernard fell into a deep sleep in his corner, and his team could not rouse him in time to begin fighting again. So Papke was declared the winner and Bernard 'retired'.

It was later claimed that the fight had been rigged and the boxer himself claimed he had been doped.

I'm sitting this one out

When the Korean flyweight Choh Dong-kih was disqualified for holding his head too low after just over a minute of the first round of a quarter-final fight during the 1964 Tokyo Olympics, he refused to accept the decision.

He was so angry, in fact, that he sat on the canvas, right in the middle of the ring, and refused to move. He remained there for fifty-one minutes before officials persuaded him to end his protest.

KO'd by emotion

Clement Quartey of Ghana did not expect to win the light-welterweight final at the 1962 Commonwealth Games in Perth. Everyone seemed convinced that Scotland's Dick McTaggart would be the victor on points.

So, when the judges awarded their decision in favour of Quartey, he was so overcome that he fainted, and was out cold on the canvas – an unusual position for a winner to be in – for about five minutes following the announcement of his victory.

More refs than fighters

Boxing referees have to be nimble on their feet, but this is to ensure they can see the fight from all angles, not to avoid blows. After all, the fighters are usually good at aiming their fists at each other, and so referees do not expect to be punched in the face. However, during a heavyweight fight held at Leicester's Granby Halls, not one, but two referees became caught in the crossfire.

Punches were flying in the ring as the two heavyweights battled to get the upper hand, and as a result of a wayward punch that landed on the hapless referee's chin, the poor man hit the canvas. Not quite knocked out, he was in no condition to continue his duties on the night. A substitute was called for, but in his enthusiasm to replace his injured colleague, the second referee tripped as he ran up the corner steps and twisted an ankle.

The bout was almost certain to be postponed until the boxing manager, George Biddles, stepped into the ring to referee the remaining rounds. Fortunately, he came to no harm, as seconds later, one of the boxers landed a knockout punch, and all Biddles had to do was count to ten.

Revealing gesture

Richard Procter, a featherweight boxer, gave his audience more than they had bargained for when he stepped smartly into the ring at the World Sporting Club in London.

Coolly he slipped off his gown and, with some aplomb, threw it into the corner to an outburst of raucous cheering. It took a few seconds for him to realize that the sudden burst of shouting, applauding and whistling was not in appreciation of his fighting prowess – after all, the bout had yet to begin. Only when he looked down did he realize he had left his shorts in the dressing room.

The bells, the bells

During the Seoul Olympics in 1988, a possible boxing knockout turned into a farce, and all because of ringing bells.

In making the decision to stage more than one fight at a time in one hall, officials had not considered the effect that the noise of more than one bell would have. How would a fighter know whether the bell he heard ringing was for his own fight or someone else's?

The inevitable happened during a light-welterweight fight between Todd Foster of the United States and Chun Jin Chul from South Korea.

Chun heard a bell and thought it referred to his own bout. Understandably, he began to walk to his corner. However, the bell had been from another fight. Foster then took advantage of the muddle, and delivered a powerful left hook to the unsuspecting Chun, knocking him to the canvas. The referee even began to count, but then seemed to realize that a mistake had been made. Confusion descended within the ring, and ultimately the judges decided it should be restaged the following day. Foster won the re-match.

Thumbs down

John Coker, a lightweight boxer from Sierra Leone, was due to take up a place in the 1966 Empire and Commonwealth Games in Kingston, Jamaica.

Unfortunately, Coker had exceptionally long thumbs, and despite endless searches, he could not find a pair of gloves to fit. As a result, he was deemed to be improperly equipped and was duly disqualified.

Weighty decision

It was a great honour for the small Pacific island of Vanuatu when it sent its only representative to the 1988 Olympics. Eduard Paululum was the island's first Olympic competitor.

Over-excited and carried away with the celebrations, he mistakenly ate a hearty breakfast before his first-round weigh-in, and was found to be just a pound overweight. In accordance with the rules he was disqualified and had to return home without having thrown a single punch.

Out – and out

Jack Doyle, the battling Irishman, ended up the loser in spite of being the favourite, when he found himself stuck outside the ring.

He was taking on Eddie Phillips in a heavyweight bout at Harringay in London in September 1938 and during the second round Doyle flew at Phillips, but missed him and continued on, through the ropes and out of the ring.

The referee began the count, but Doyle could not get back in time, and was counted out. Phillips was the surprise – and surprised – victor.

Photo finish

Adolpho Washington had already suffered a cut eye during his WBA light-heavyweight title fight against the defender Virgil Hill in February 1993.

Between the twelfth and thirteenth rounds at Fargo, North Dakota, Washington was having his eye checked by a doctor at the ringside, when an overenthusiastic cameraman went in for a good close-up. In his excitement, the cameraman hit Washington's eye with his camera, and it began to bleed even more. Consequently, Washington was unable to continue.

Seconds away

At just half a second long, it must have been the shortest fight on record. It was ten and a half seconds, more accurately, but ten of those comprised the count following Ralph Walton's knockout by Al Couture at Lewiston, Maine, in September 1946.

Walton was still adjusting his gum shield when Couture punched him on the jaw, knocking him to the canvas, where he lay, out cold.

Count me in

Few boxers can claim they have been on the canvas for more than ten seconds but have still been able to continue fighting. On 22 September 1927 in Chicago, Jack Dempsey lost to Gene Tunney, who retained his world heavyweight title, after a controversial incident occurred.

Dempsey knocked Tunney to the canvas, but the referee, Dave Barry, would not begin the count until Dempsey had gone into a neutral corner. He eventually had to usher him there, which extended the time the prone Tunney could remain on the canvas.

He was allowed to continue, despite having lain on the canvas for fourteen seconds before the count reached nine. He recovered enough to win on points, thus retaining his title.

The fight has since become known as the Battle of the Long Count.

Self-defeat (1)

Poor Daniel Caruso thought he was performing the perfect warm-up when he began pounding his gloves into his own face before the introductions in the New York Golden Gloves Championships in January 1992. It was just a psyching-up exercise. Nothing unusual in that. But Dan punched himself hard on the nose, breaking and bloodying it, and doctors decided he was unfit to fight.

Self-defeat (2)

On the occasion of a regional heat of the Saginaw Golden Gloves Championships in Michigan in 1977, Harvey Gartley and Dennis Outlette were advised by their teams to be cautious on their boxing debut: avoid throwing any wild punches, size up their man for a while, take it slowly.

Forty-seven seconds into the fight, neither man had managed to land a punch, so the crowd were growing restless. Gartley sensed the crowd's impatience, forgot his orders and panicked, launching a swing towards Outlette. Unfortunately, he failed to make contact with his opponent, and the energy with which he had thrown himself into the punch simply caused him to collapse on to the canvas and be counted out.

Slugging it out (of jail)

A former WBC lightweight champion slipped up by not paying the arrears in his child support, and was jailed for it. Then he had to be released from jail in order to earn the money to pay.

In 2002 Stevie Johnston was jailed on 25 March for contempt of court, having failed to pay three women – the mothers of four of his children – about £96,000 in child support over eighteen months.

At a Denver hearing, the twenty-nine-year-old fighter agreed to pay the three women an undisclosed sum of money immediately, and give them part of his purse from a forthcoming fight in Las Vegas and, in exchange, a judge ordered him to be released so he could train for said fight.

When Irish eyes were crying

Northern Ireland's Wayne McCullough was not usually given to outpourings of emotion at the sound of the national anthem, not even when standing proudly on a podium receiving a gold medal.

At the 1990 Commonwealth Games in Auckland, however, after McCullough had won the flyweight title, and been presented with the gold medal, the national anthem could not be played, owing to a technical problem with the tape machine.

In an effort to fill the embarrassing silence, a games official called Bob Gibson picked up the microphone and sang 'Danny Boy'. Before long the whole crowd had joined in. McCullough was apparently so moved that it was all he could do to fight back the tears.

Bobby's fall to fame

A sure-fire way of slipping up in the world of sport is to disagree with those who sit – or stand – in judgement. Bobby Frankham, a light-heavyweight, refused to accept the decision of referee Richie Davies to stop his fight with Billy Sims of Hackney in the first round at Wembley in December 1987.

He was so much in disagreement with Davies that he made him his next opponent, and swung punches at him. Having twice hit the referee in the face, he decided to target Sims's corner men, and then start an unofficial second round with Sims himself.

It was then the rival fans' turn, with the result that the referee needed a police escort to accompany him from the ring. The British Boxing Board of Control said it was an 'utterly disgraceful' episode, and Frankham said, 'I just had a brainstorm,' adding that it was 'a bad way to get famous'.

Pre-fight fight

Boxers are particularly sensitive about their 'manhood', it seems, but this curious notion led to a fight before the fight in 1994, when the WBO champion Michael Bentt and his challenger Herbie Hide from Norwich brawled at a photocall.

A woman had put a Millwall baseball cap on Bentt's head, but Hide knocked it off and said, 'I want a Norwich cap.' Bentt then hit him in the head and within seconds they were aiming punches at each other while officials and handlers tried to intervene and bring peace to the proceedings.

Both men were judged equally to blame by the British Boxing Board of Control and were each fined £10,000. Bentt said of the fine, 'You don't get anything for fighting outside the ring, but he compromised my manhood.'

Ref put his foot in it

After a fight against Liverpool's Nel Tarleton, in which he was defending his British featherweight title at Anfield in October 1931, Sheffield's Johnny Cuthbert moaned, 'Losing the title was bad enough, but it didn't half rub it in when I realized I'd been beaten by a bloke with one lung and only one foot!'

Things began to go wrong when the referee, while going in to break the men up, trod heavily on Tarleton's foot, causing much pain. The foot continued to throb for the next five rounds, as the Liverpool man hobbled around and the Sheffielder took full advantage.

Tarleton was not only challenged mobility-wise, but he also had only one lung, and yet won the match on points.

Farr far away

One of the best-known names in British boxing in the 1950s was Tommy Farr, who became the British heavyweight champion.

When he was still nineteen, Farr fought Eddie Steele of Norwood at Crystal Palace, having been called up as a last-minute replacement.

All was going well for Farr, until Steele jabbed him in the throat. The punch had a bizarre effect on Farr, who bolted from the ring and fled to the dressing room. Even years later he would not give an explanation of this unusual behaviour.

Frankly speaking ...

The radio reporter must have wanted to get the bare facts – or perhaps the naked truth – when he approached Frank Bruno at the Royal Albert Hall.

The encounter took place after Bruno had dealt with Larry Frazier in two rounds. Bruno had just come out of the shower in the dressing room and was stark naked, dripping wet and heading for his clothes. The reporter shoved the microphone under his nose and asked, 'What do you plan to do next?'

Bruno, quick as a right hook, replied, 'Hopefully dry myself and get some clothes on.'

'Don't you feel it's time you were exposed to somebody in the top ten, so we can see what you're really made of?' asked the reporter.

Bruno looked down at himself and delivered his verbal KO: 'Well, if you don't know now, nobody will.'

Then came his deep laugh as he added, after the microphone had been switched off, 'It's just as well that interview wasn't on television – know what I mean?'

The disappearing ref

Tom Sayers of London and John C. Heenan of the United States had met for a bare-knuckle fight at Farnborough in Kent in April 1860, and had gone for thirty-seven hard rounds when it looked as though Sayers was going to be beaten.

However, one of his supporters in the crowd had the bright idea of cutting the ropes to cause the match to be abandoned. Police and spectators spilled into the ring and there was mayhem. Eventually, the situation was brought to order, but the referee had disappeared. He remained absent for another five rounds, during which the two men fought on without him.

When he did return, he declared the match a draw.

A-bob-bob-bobbin' along

A barge was the chosen venue for the WBC bantamweight title fight between Antonio Avelar of Mexico and Miguel Lora of Colombia in July 1987.

The vessel was moored in Miami's Marine Stadium, but although it was firmly anchored to the sea bed, the ring did more bobbing up and down than the boxers' gloves and heads.

Crowd trouble

Sometimes it is the spectators who are responsible for the sporting slip-up, and never more so than in August 1815 during a bare-knuckle fight on Blackheath, London, between London's Caleb Baldwin, a former England champion, and an Irishman, Bill Ryan.

In what was to be his last bout, Baldwin was exhausted by the twenty-sixth round and slumped to the ground. But Ryan hit him while he was on his knees to cries of 'Foul!' by Baldwin's supporters.

A free-for-all ensued among the crowd, and the Dragoon

Guards had to be called to calm things down. By this time, however, the ring had been wrecked and the contest was declared a draw.

And in the tight corner ...

Sometimes the weather contributes to the sporting slip-up, as in the case of the 1988 European bantamweight match between the reigning champion, Cincenzo Belcastro of Italy, and Britain's Billy Hardy.

The bout had been due to take place in a large marquee that had been erected in Fuscaldo, southern Italy, the champion's home town. Unfortunately, the marquee was wrecked by a gusty wind, so the contest had to be transferred to a sports hall in nearby Paola.

The sports hall was so inadequate that the spectators were packed in like sardines, leading one sportswriter to comment, 'The only people seated comfortably were the fighters.'

Belcastro won by a small margin.

Boxing not so clever

Referees are used to dodging and weaving so they can get a view of the action from all possible angles, but in May 1948, Joey Walker got too close to the action and was knocked out cold.

Walker had been refereeing a welterweight contest between Mike De Cosmo of the United States and Laurie Buxton of Watford at Newark in New Jersey.

Buxton aimed to hit De Cosmo's head, but missed, and the glove hit the referee squarely on the jaw. He did get up, eventually, but was unable to continue and a substitute was brought in.

Walker said, 'I guess I can't take a punch like I used to.'

Down, but not out

It is hard to believe, but even after knocking out an opponent it is still possible to lose a fight, as Joe Lazarus, the US bantamweight, proved in the 1924 Paris Olympics.

Oscar Andren of Sweden was being revived after he had been knocked down and counted out, only to learn that he had *won* the match. Lazarus, apparently, had been hitting Andren during a clinch just a few seconds before the knockout, which led to his disqualification.

Swedish team officials, wishing to be seen to be the epitome of fairness, even offered a rematch, so embarrassed were they at seeing their man knocked out and yet winning – but officials said no. Andren was declared the winner.

Dark deeds

When John Knifton and Tom Scutton met in London in August 1877 for a world heavyweight title fight, a brawl broke out among the crowd during the ninth round. As the owner of the venue was growing increasingly worried about the safety of his property, he decided to turn out the gas lights, plunging the entire venue into darkness.

In minutes peace had been restored, but when the lights came back on the referee, a Mr J. Jenn, was missing. In the confusion he had left and gone home.

He didn't take it sitting down

Modern-day boxers have an easy life, it would seem, with a cosy canvas to fall on, bouncy ropes, soft gloves, warm hall, Queensberry Rules, and someone to stop the fight if one fighter is causing too much damage to the other.

Two hundred years ago, boxers had far less protection. On 12 May 1789 a bare-knuckle fight in Surrey took place between

'Gentleman' John Jackson and George Inglestone, but torrential rain had turned the ring into a virtual skating rink, with the fighters sliding around like ice-dancers, but not nearly so gracefully.

It is unusual for a boxer to break his leg in a fight, but that was just what Jackson managed to do when he fell, and he also dislocated an ankle.

He was determined to continue with the fight, however, and offered to be strapped into a chair so that he could do just that. Inglestone was not as enthusiastic, so the fight came to an end.

Tooth and jaw

During a bare-knuckle fight between two English-born fighters in Canada back in 1872, Billy Edwards took on Arthur Chambers in a world lightweight title fight at Squirrel Island. Although Chambers was being soundly beaten, he conned the referee into giving him the match on account of a foul.

When he came out for the twenty-sixth round he screamed that his opponent had bitten him. When the referee, Bill Tracy, saw the teeth marks on Chambers's face, he had no choice but to declare the incident a foul, and award the match to Chambers.

What Tracy was completely unaware of, though, was that Chambers's second, Tom Allen, had been doing the biting between rounds because he could see that his man would never have won by following the rules.

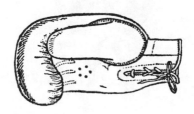

A weighty decision

Though comfort eating can bring short-term happiness, it was by far the wrong option for a South African lightweight boxer named Thomas Hamilton-Brown at the Berlin Olympics in 1936.

Upset that he had lost a split decision to his opponent, Carlos Lillo of Chile, he decided to cheer himself up with a binge, but it transpired that he had not lost the fight after all, because one of the judges had reversed the scores in error.

When Hamilton-Brown's manager went to tell him the good news, the forlorn fighter had already put on 5 pounds (2.25 kilos) in weight and was over the limit for the next bout, and was disqualified from the competition.

Hair today ...

When the Argentine bantamweight Arnoldo Pares was still over the required weight, something had to come off. Since he was only marginally above the required poundage, his team decided to cut off his hair, but it was still not enough, and officials protested when he remained a few ounces over the limit. Eventually though, it was discovered that the scales had been wrong all along, and so poor old Pares had lost his lovely locks for nothing.

The Leather and the Willow

Of all the games that people choose to make fun of, cricket must be the most lampooned. Imagine the confusion of the imaginary man from Mars who stumbles on to a green field on a sunny afternoon in rural England. Knowing something of the language, he hears talk of a 'maiden over' and 'silly mid-off', then glancing up at the scoreboard, is totally bamboozled and bemused as the game goes on for three, four or five days.

While many countries play cricket and consider it one of their national sports, there is something quintessentially English about it, somehow. Not surprisingly, this great sport gives rise to a number of mishaps, blunders and humorous moments, of which a great many are featured here:

Close call
Brian Close was fielding in a match between Gloucestershire and Yorkshire in July 1962, and Gloucestershire's Martin Young was batting. Ray Illingworth bowled, and Young hit it to short leg, where Brian Close took it on the temple, and it bounced to Phil Sharpe, who caught it at first slip.

Close was asked by a worried team-mate what would have happened if the ball had hit him right between the eyes. With a touch of nonchalance, Close replied, 'He'd have been caught at cover.'

Dirigible danger

Few grounds can boast that play has been stopped by a hot-air balloon and a runaway car. It happened at Curdridge's ground in Hampshire in 1982 and 1997 respectively.

In 1982, the hot-air balloon was promoting a new burger bar, and it ran out of fuel, landing on the pitch during Curdridge's match against their fellow Hampshire side Medstead.

In 1997, eighty-year-old Grace Cummins's Vauxhall Astra went out of control when its elderly driver got her foot stuck between the brake and accelerator pedals. The car tore around the ground during Curdridge's match with Denmead, and hit three other cars and a player's wife. Eventually, Ms Cummins managed to release her foot, and play resumed some time later.

Another incident involving a runaway car at Beaconsfield Cricket Club in Buckinghamshire, in July 1992, led to the abandonment of the match.

Four spectators were hurt as the car, driven by the eighty-six-year-old club president, Tom Orford, shot across the pitch. He had come to present the prizes.

Empty wicket

Communication breakdowns happen in all sports, but sometimes they are funnier than others.

During a match in South Africa, Bobby Simpson was captaining Australia. With a lead of 450, his team were very much in the driving seat by teatime. During the twenty-minute break, Simpson forgot to tell the opposing captain that he wished to enforce the follow-on. So, after tea, both teams came out to field.

Hard to swallow – but true

SBW is a new situation similar to LBW, but means 'swallow before wicket'. It is a rare event, but two instances of the phenomenon have been recorded in the cricketing annals.

The first occasion was in November 1969, when South Australia's Greg Chappell bowled to John Inverarity of Western Australia. The ball hit a swallow in midair, and was deflected on to the stumps. The umpire decided it was a no-ball.

At Trimdon, County Durham in 1994, a similar incident occurred when Chris Thomas's ball hit a swallow in flight and was deflected on to the stumps of the batsman, Joe Hall. The umpires conferred and ruled that the ball was dead. So was the swallow.

The LBW initials were more appropriate during the First Test between Young Sri Lanka and Young England in 1987. Play was stopped when a large iguana wandered in front of the wicket at the ground at Colombo Cricket Club – a case of Lizard Before Wicket.

Farce in the grass

When Richard Johnson was batting for the Jesters CC against Totteridge in 1975, he hit a powerful six that soared into the air and hit a spectator's car that was parked in a grassy field. A young man suddenly appeared from the long grass, having been lying in the private spot with a young lady.

Hearing the ball land on his car with a resounding thud, he had stood up hurriedly to demand what had happened. The seriousness of his enquiry was lost on the nearby spectators and outfield cricketers, however, as his trousers promptly fell down around his ankles.

Fiery performance

The scorebook could well have read, 'Run out while fighting fire', as that is what actually happened to Stan Dawson, who was batting at Kalgoorlie in Australia in the 1970s.

A quick delivery was bowled that hit him on his hip pocket which contained a box of matches. In an astonishing fluke, some of the matches ignited.

It was while Stan was leaping around beating down the flames with his hands that his opponents ran him out.

Heading for a catch

The Bishop Auckland professional Ricky Waldren completed a straight drive in a match in July 1995, but did not expect to be caught out in quite such an odd manner.

The ball collided with the head of George Simpson, the umpire at the bowler's end, and was caught by an opposing fielder right out on the boundary.

Simpson went to hospital. Waldren went to the pavilion.

Giving it their best shot

It was the first ball of the match when Bunbury of Western Australia were at home to a touring team from Victoria in the late-nineteenth century. The visiting side's opening batsman banged the ball right into a tree, where it became stuck.

The batsmen began to run ...

Fielders tried in vain to get the ball out of the tree while the batsmen continued to run.

The next ploy was to look for an axe to fell the tree, but meanwhile the batsmen ran and ran – and ran some more … Finally, somebody produced a rifle, and shot down the offending ball, by which time the batsmen, doubtless shattered after their exertions, had scored 286 runs.

In for a penny?
In his test debut for England against Australia at Lord's in 1975, David Steele was naturally a bit nervous.

As he set off from the dressing room, bound for the field of play, he descended an extra flight of steps in error and ended up in the pavilion toilets.

Great Scott!
While Clive Scott's wife wheeled their baby around the field during a 1994 club match, she was hit on the head by a ball that had been hit for six by her own husband.

Heads you lose …
In the 1996 Ranji Trophy semi-final in Madras between Tamil Nadu and Delhi, they argued the toss to such an extent that most of the first morning's play was lost.

The row was over which face of a newly introduced coin was heads and which was tails. The umpires offered a second toss, but Delhi's Ajoy Sharma refused. He did finally agree – after two hours – and won the toss, but his team went on to lose by eight wickets.

Hit for two

Gloucestershire's Andrew Symonds did not have anything personal against the female spectator. She was, after all, a Gloucestershire supporter. However, he did ensure that she twice needed treatment for her injuries.

She was enjoying the match between Sussex and Gloucestershire at Hove in June 1995 when, during Symonds's first innings, a powerful four left the ground and hit her in the face. Off she went for treatment, but was enjoying the cricket again when a Symonds' six made painful contact with her leg.

Home and away

Entire books are written about cricket tours, but one was not all that it seemed. E. H. D. Sewell's *From a Window at Lord's* describes the MCC's 1936–37 tour to Australia, written as soon as the tour ended. Strangely, though, the author had never left England.

Ian's X file

Not all sporting slip-ups occur on the field of play. Ian Greig, the England cricketer, had to go to hospital for an X-ray after he had hurt his hand in a match against Pakistan in 1987, and it was confirmed that he had a fracture in a finger bone.

It was not such a bad break, and he was likely to recover quickly, but as he stood to leave, he banged his head on the X-ray machine, leaving him with a wound needing two stitches.

In for a duck?

It is unlikely that any cricket ground these days can boast a pond. In 1922, the ground at Malton, Yorkshire, could when the cricket team was visited by its neighbours, Scarborough.

The pond was just beyond the boundary rope in one corner,

and the man batting was a big hitter called Charles Inglis Thornton – the type of batsman able to push fields further and further out.

Thornton was also able to get shots between the fielders, until he hit the ball very close to one of them on the boundary. The unfortunate fellow thought the ball might just clear his head, so he ran backwards, trying to make a catch.

The inevitable happened, of course, and into the pond he went.

Here come da Judge (quack, quack!)

Many a cricketer has experienced the humiliation of being bowled for a duck. To be bowled for two first-ball ducks in successive balls – and in the same match – is quite an achievement, however, and it happened to the Glamorgan tailender Peter Judge in 1946.

After being the last man out against the Indian tourists, he was bowled first ball by the leg spinner Chandra Sarwate. Time was running out, and India decided to enforce the follow-on.

The Glamorgan captain signalled to Judge to remain in the middle to start the next innings. The bowler was once again Sarwate, who managed to clean-bowl the hapless Judge with the first ball.

Into the long grass

It is not only golf balls that disappear into the long grass; cricket balls do, too.

When Macleod played against Banyale in a Victoria country match at Windsor Reserve in 1990, Garry Chapman, the Banyale batsman, hit the ball to mid-wicket and it went into grass of about 25 centimetres in height. The batsmen scored seventeen runs while the fielders searched for it.

It all ended in tears

At a first-class cricket match between England and the West Indies at Sabina Park in Kingston, Jamaica, things got out of hand when the crowd became rather annoyed about the dismissal of one of the West Indian batsmen, Basil Butcher.

They began to hurl bottles on to the pitch and one hit the England captain, Colin Cowdrey, on the foot. He appealed for them to calm down, but his words either could not be heard or they fell on deaf ears.

So the police entered the fray, and sprayed the crowd with tear gas. Unfortunately, they had not checked the wind direction first, and so the gas drifted off into the pavilion. It travelled further than the pavilion too, and was carried on the wind into the parliament building, where the Cabinet was in session, forcing a premature suspension of proceedings.

Just the ticket

Ilfracombe Rugby Club ground at Hele in Devon sits on a steep hill, which can make life rather difficult for fielders at times when cricket is played there.

Paul Crabb was playing for the club's cricket section against a neighbouring team, Woolacombe, in July 1996, when a ball was hit out of the ground.

Crabb chased it, but it bounced onto a road, and the road was

a hill, and the ball began to roll.

Crabb followed in hot pursuit – 100 yards, 200 yards, 300 yards, eventually a quarter of a mile away from the ground before the ball finally came to a halt.

He was about to turn round and run back up the hill to return to the match, but a bus arrived and when he told the driver what had happened, the tired fielder was offered a free ride.

In similar circumstances in 1997, a ball that was hit out of the ground during a match between schools from Macclesfield and Bangor, landed on a passing lorry and was never seen again.

Just thought I'd drop in ...

Whether it was a spectator who had failed to get a ticket and wanted a bird's-eye view of the match, in April 1997 a fielder was hit by a hang-glider while fielding close to the boundary, during a friendly match between his side Horncastle and a team from Bardney.

Other players dragged the smashed glider off the field so the game could continue, while the pilot explained that he had been trying to avoid a crop field.

The injured fielder, John Hague, was left nursing a sore head.

Huffing and puffing

Robin Wightman was a bit annoyed when his captain refused to allow him to bowl the final over. It was an understandable reaction as Robin, who was playing for Whiteleas against East Rainton in the North East Durham League in August 1995, had already taken seven wickets.

His captain would not back down, so Wightman stormed off the pitch and would not return.

When Whiteleas went in to bat, Wightman's departure was recorded in the scorebook as 'absent, huffed'.

Out!

It seems that scorers do not mince words when the reasons for a cricketer's absence must be accurately recorded and displayed.

In the case of Abdul Aziz, who was injured in the first innings of the final of the 1958–59 Qaid-I-Azam Trophy in Karachi, the scorecard read, 'Abdul Aziz retired hurt ... 0'.

The injury proved to be fatal, however, so the scorer wrote for the second innings, 'Abdul Aziz did not bat, dead ... 0'.

Snow joke

When Leicestershire batsman Paul Marner saw the ball crumble after it had made contact with his bat, he could be excused for thinking he had soap in his eyes, because he probably had.

The 'ball' had come from the hand of England and Sussex fast bowler John Snow, causing Marner to go on to his back foot to hook what seemed like a loose full toss. The 'ball' shattered into a myriad pieces, however, causing the Sussex team to fall about laughing. Snow had delivered a bar of red soap, and told the local press that day that he was launching a 'clean up cricket' campaign.

Machine madness

A bowler would doubtless show some compassion if a batsman was down, despite being on opposing sides; not so a bowling machine.

It was during the winter of 1985-86 and Martyn Goulding of Torquay had decided to hone his batting skills with the help of a bowling machine.

Things were going well until the machine sent a 75-m.p.h. delivery, which hit Martyn's foot, and broke it. But while he was down on the ground, gripping his foot in agony, the machine continued its relentless assault, and down came another fast delivery, which hit him in the chest and broke two ribs.

The ups and downs of it

At the end of the 1996 Mercantile Mutual Insurance Cup tie with New South Wales in Sydney, South Australia left the field thinking they had lost the fifty-over match by a run, but it was discovered that the scorers had not taken account of a no-ball in the forty-eighth over, and so the two extra runs turned their defeat into a three-wicket victory.

The New South Wales team, by contrast, were less impressed with their short-lived triumph.

No-ball!

An important piece of equipment was missing when Derbyshire and Shropshire were poised to do battle in a NatWest Trophy match at Chesterfield in June 1990.

Someone had forgotten to bring the match balls, so a new batch had to be sent for from county headquarters in Derby, delaying the start of the match by forty-five minutes.

Not so funny bone

The Darfield team were cock-a-hoop when their wicketkeeper, Gavin Roebuck, stumped an opponent in a Barnsley Sunday League match in 1996.

Indeed, they were so thrilled with the efforts of their colleague that they were a little too rough when congratulating him, and managed to break his elbow.

Oh, Doctor ...

It is unlikely that Dr R. L. Park was ever picked again after his performance in 1920. He was selected to play for Australia against England in Melbourne, but failed to impress. Not only was he out first ball when it was his turn to bat but, when it was his turn to bowl, he completed just one over costing nine runs.

Stumped!

The South African Under-19s team and the Transvaal Colts were playing at the Correctional Services ground in Pretoria in 1994, but the game had to be reduced from fifty-five overs a side to fifty.

The reason was that the start had been delayed because the stumps were missing, presumed stolen.

On me 'ead, sun

England's all-rounder Chris Lewis decided on a new image for the 1993–94 tour of the West Indies. Whether it was for reasons of vanity or in an effort to keep him cool, he decided to shave his head completely, transforming his appearance.

Unfortunately, though, he forgot to wear his hat and got sunstroke.

Pockets and sockets

The World Series match at Colombo between Sri Lanka and Zimbabwe in 1996 had to be delayed for eight minutes because no one could find the bails. They were eventually located in the groundsman's pocket.

In 1975, one of the rarest possibilities in cricket occurred at a County Championship match between Leicestershire and Lancashire. The Leicestershire wicketkeeper, Barry Dudleston, stumped the Lancashire batsman, David Lloyd, but the bails leaped up off the stumps and landed right back in position in their sockets. Lloyd took full advantage of this extraordinary reprieve, and made a century.

In Chile, in 1922, another pocket was at the heart of a strange occurrence. A batsman was given out at Valparaiso Cricket Club after his drive landed in the pocket of a white cardigan worn by a fielder.

Strictly for the Bird

When Dickie Bird was overseeing a match at Northampton, Allan Lamb came in to bat and handed his mobile phone to the famous umpire, saying, 'Look after this for me, please, Dickie. I didn't want to leave it in the dressing room.'

After about five minutes' play, Lamb's phone began chirping and Bird, realizing it was not a small feathered creature that was making the noise, had no alternative but to answer it. To his bemusement, Ian Botham was at the end of the line, calling to ask for the score.

For Dickie Bird, this was not the first time technology had distracted him from the more sedate music of willow on leather. On one occasion at Bournemouth, during his playing days with Yorkshire, he was due to face a ball against Hampshire when his attention was diverted. He was sure he could hear the frenetic tones of a racing commentary, and he noticed that over in the slips Colin Ingleby-Mackenzie had a transistor radio pressed to his ear.

'Hope I'm not breaking your concentration, old chap,' Mackenzie called out. 'I've got a few bob riding on a nag.'

Technology also led to a ban on a former Pakistan test

cricketer, Parvez Mir by the Carrow club of Norfolk in 1995. He had interrupted the bowling to take a call from his fiancée on his mobile phone – right in the middle of an over. The umpire had been looking after the instrument, and Mir took it from him to chat. He then handed it back and continued his bowling.

Pyrrhic victory

It was a long way to the boundary for David O'Sullivan, who was fielding for New Zealand in the First Test of the 1973–74 series in Australia. Off he went in pursuit of a rolling ball, hoping to reach it before it went over the boundary for a four.

After a full-length dive, he stopped the ball just before it rolled over the rope. However, in the time it had taken him to get to the boundary, do the dive, pick up the ball and throw it, the batsmen had run five.

Rain stopped, play began

When rain stopped play on the last day of the County Championship match between Hampshire and Glamorgan in June 1969, there were two hours left at the Bournemouth ground, and an early finish to the match looked inevitable.

So the Hampshire players left the ground to return to their respective homes, as the match, as far as they knew, had been abandoned. The rain stopped, however, and play resumed, or it would have done had the Hampshire team returned.

Glamorgan's men entered the field and remained for the regulation two minutes before being awarded a win by the umpires.

All was not lost, however. The MCC, which arbitrates in such matters, decided the Hampshire side were victims of a misunderstanding, and rescinded the umpires' decision.

Reined in by rain

Sidney Wells had been looking forward to this day. At last, in 1927, he was selected for his first – and only – first-class match. It was against Kent.

The British weather got the better of the occasion, though, and the match was deluged. Not a ball was bowled. Poor Sid was out of first-class cricket before he had even got in.

Too, too bad

South Africa's top Anglican cleric, Archbishop Desmond Tutu, wanted to visit the dressing room at tea on the first day of the First Test at Lord's in July 1994, when his country's team was making its first appearance in England for twenty-nine years.

He had not counted on the strict attitude of the Lord's stewards, however, who stopped him from entering the pavilion because he was not wearing a jacket.

Revolutionary!

It was to be the first overseas cricket tour. The date was August 1789, the year of the French Revolution. The England team were about to go to Paris for a fixture organized by the Duke of Dorset, a major player in the cricketing world of the time, and also the British ambassador in Paris at the start of the Revolution.

The team travelled to Dover ready for the Channel crossing, having been told they would have safe passage, in spite of the troubles. However, before they could embark, they saw none other than the Duke himself, fleeing Paris.

In the interests of safety, a decision was made to abandon the match.

Ribbet, ribbet!

It was a strange old wicket for the final Test during England's tour of South Africa in 1922–23. The ball stopped almost dead after it had been pitched. When batsmen tentatively prodded the wicket they did not find a natural irregularity such as a bump in the ground, but a pile of small green frogs.

Play was suspended so that they could be removed for their own safety.

Try this, Ian!

Ian Botham was the next man to bat and was on his approach to the wicket when England were touring Western Australia in 1986–87. But there was something missing, which Botham was completely unaware of until the twelfth man tapped him on his shoulder, proffered one of those things made of willow with a handle that cricketers use to hit a ball with, and suggested it would be rather useful.

Botham had been so keen to join the action that he had left his bat behind.

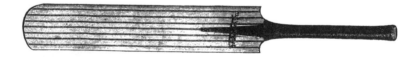

Setting an example

In the early 1960s, Jon Fellows-Smith, the South African captain of Northamptonshire, was adamant that the wet wicket was perfectly safe to play on. However, his pace men were a bit reluctant to open the bowling. The pitch, they claimed, was just too dangerous.

Fellows-Smith decided to set an example to his players, but slipped on his run-up and had to be taken to hospital with a broken ankle.

Squids in

When two South African teams, Border and Boland, played each other in February 1995, Border's Daryll Cullinan hit a six. The ball landed right in the calamari, a squid dish, being cooked in a frying pan.

It was fished out, but it was several minutes before it was cool enough to be washed clean of the grease, which was not entirely removed, but the ball remained slippery, and eventually a replacement had to be provided.

The spilling fields

In the 1975–76 Test series between the West Indies and India, Clive Lloyd made 70 in the Second Test, allowing the West Indies to achieve a draw, and gain a series win against India 2–1.

However, Lloyd would not have made such a score had it not been for the enthusiasm of two fielders as he sent the ball towards mid-off. Eknath Solkar and Brijesh Patel went to catch it at the same time neither, it seems, aware of the other's presence. The midair collision was inevitable, and the ball landed on the grass, leaving Lloyd still at the crease.

The Winslow boys

There are numerous stories about teams who, for one reason or another, fail to turn up for a match, but it is quite something when each of two teams finds itself playing against the wrong opponents.

In June 1996, a Buckinghamshire club called Winslow Town were due to play against a Bedfordshire team named Kempston. They were expecting to play Kempston Ramblers but, owing to a communication slip-up, they found themselves playing against Kempston Meltis, because the team due to play Kempston Meltis had not shown up either.

No one actually knew they were playing at the wrong ground until one of the Ramblers players, who had gone in search of the Winslow Town team, found them and took them to the right venue.

When Winslow's batsman, Ron Phillips, was asked why he had failed to spot the error, he said at the time, 'I've played against Ramblers a number of times over the years, and I thought all their batsmen must have retired or died off.'

To cap it all ...

M. J. K. Smith was about to take a ball from Hampshire at Edgbaston in 1962, when a gust of wind took his cap off and it landed on the wicket. The former Warwickshire and England captain was given out, 'hit wicket'.

Tooth decay

In April 1997, while Brian Lucas was rolling the hallowed turf at the Perkins Cricket Club in Shropshire, he sneezed and his false teeth shot out.

Unable to stop the machine in time, the roller went over the prized dentures, and crushed them beyond recognition, leaving Lucas sans teeth.

What's the buzz?

Bees stopped play in May 1997 when Helston and Falmouth faced each other in a Cornwall League First Division match.

Thousands of them had swarmed on to the field, and two players were stung. Beekeeping experts were called in to remove the intruders.

Where there's smoke, there's pyre

A match at Boddington in Gloucestershire had to be abandoned in 1995, because of dead animals.

The problem was that the pitch was covered in smoke from the nearby Companion's Rest pet crematorium at Elmstone Hardwicke.

Wrong again, Chinmay

A would-be MCC player, Chinmay Gupte, travelled all the way to Blackheath in Greater London in order to play for the top side. However, he had gone to the wrong Blackheath; he should have travelled to Surrey.

Desperate not to make the same mistake the following year, he went to Blackheath, Surrey, only to be told he should have turned up at Blackheath, London.

Yes! By that I mean no!

Should we? Shouldn't we? It can sometimes be a difficult decision whether to make the run or stay put. Godfrey Evans, an England wicketkeeper, made an entertaining run during the Third Test against Australia at Sydney in the 1950–51 Ashes series.

Evans set off to run, but got Doug Wright run out after sending him back and then changing his mind.

This stop-go performance eventually cost England the game by an innings and thirteen runs, because poor old Wright, in trying to respond to his colleague's equivocation, pulled a groin muscle and that put paid to his bowling for the rest of the match.

You must be choking!

Australia had declared on 729 for 6, leaving England facing a first-innings deficit of 304 in the Second Test at Lord's in 1930.

Percy Chapman had reached 121 when a bluebottle flew into his mouth, causing him to choke. Coughing madly, he was caught behind, not having added to his score. Australia went on to win by seven wickets.

Sheep stop play

In Ebbw Vale, in 1948, Glamorgan's county match against Gloucestershire was progressing nicely until play had to be stopped when a flock of sheep decided that the grass on the cricket field was better than their usual grazing area.

Sheep are not the only animals to halt a match. Only nine months before the incident in Wales, South Australia were playing Queensland when the game was stopped after thousands of grasshoppers descended upon the pitch.

In 1962 a swarm of bees were unwelcome visitors at the Parks, during a match between Oxford University and Worcestershire.

Players get the hump

Animals of a more exotic nature have been known to put a stop to cricket matches. In the match between Launceston and Old Suttonians in August 1984, play had to be stopped on four occasions because a herd of camels wandered on to the pitch; they had strayed from a nearby circus.

Alarming disappointment

In July 1997, Philip North was called up for the first time in eight years by Glamorgan, and was looking forward to the match against Nottinghamshire in the County Championship at Colwyn Bay. However, North – a left-arm spinner and captain of the Wales Minor Counties team – overslept and turned up late for the match. So his dream of playing for

Glamorgan was shattered, because he was dropped from the side for his tardiness. His excuse to officials was that his early-morning alarm call had been forgotten.

On the card

It can safely be said that New Zealand did not acquit themselves well at Auckland in March 1955 when they played England. The scorecard reveals why:

J. G. Leggatt	1
M. B. Poore	0
B. Sutcliffe	11
J. R. Reid	1
G. O. Rathbone	7
S. N. McGregor	1
H. B. Cave	5
A. R. MacGibbon	0
I. A. Colquhoun	0
A. M. Moir not out	0
J. A. Hayes	0
Extras	0
Total	26

England played quite dismally, in fact, winning by only an innings and twenty runs.

A shattering experience

In 1985 at Holton-Le-Clay, Dennis Lovesey, who lived near the local cricket ground, had grown so tired of spectators' cars blocking access to his house, he drove his lorry on to the pitch and parked it right in the middle, refusing to move it.

Eventually, officials prevailed upon him to move the vehicle after they had appealed to the offending drivers to stop blocking Mr Lovesey's drive.

According to a report in the cricketer's bible, Wisden, a similar incident occurred eight years later. A lorry driver was so enraged after a six had flown out of the cricket ground at Wansford, near Peterborough, and shattered his windscreen, that he parked his lorry on the pitch. He would not move until insurance details had been exchanged.

A smashing six

Cricket balls have been known to go through car windows, especially at small grounds where players' and spectators' cars may well be within a well-batted six of the crease. But the impact of the ball bowled by Walsden cricketer Peter Green, had a more personal touch.

When he delivered the ball to Rochdale's Wilson Hartley in a Central Lancashire League match, Hartley whacked the ball with his accustomed gusto and off it went for a soaring six, right into an adjoining street and through the window of a house – Peter Green's house.

Bowled out of a decent benefit

Sometimes it does not pay to be too good at one's job. Bertie Buse was a Somerset all-rounder whose benefit match took place against Lancashire in 1953. The pitch was rather perky and so after the Somerset team had been bowled out for fifty-five runs, Buse decided to put his fiery bowling into action.

He took six wickets and Lancashire were bowled out for 158. Somerset came in again, but fared little better and were out for seventy-nine runs, leaving Lancashire the winners by an innings and twenty-four runs.

Ironically, it was Buse's bowling prowess that had meant that the match was over in the first day, which was of no financial benefit to Buse's benefit match.

A costly drop

In June 1994, players and spectators at the Warwickshire v Durham game at Edgbaston witnessed one of the costliest dropped catches of all time. Warwickshire's Brian Lara had made just eighteen runs, and sent what appeared to be a simple catch to the Durham wicketkeeper, Chris Scott. Lara realized his error and had started his walk back to the pavilion, but Scott dropped it.

Feeling thoroughly infuriated with himself, the wicketkeeper sighed, 'I suppose he'll go on and get a century now.' How wrong he was, for Lara went on to make not one century but five, finishing on 501 not out.

It's just not cricket!

Thomas White of Reigate in Surrey was bowled out quite often and, understandably, did not appreciate it. One day in September 1771 he turned up for a game between the Chertsey club and Hambledon with a cricket bat that was much wider than the wicket.

There are rules to prevent such activity now, but in 1771, Mr White's opponents were left completely stumped.

Written off

Former England all-rounder Derek Pringle did not sustain his back injury after twisting awkwardly to catch the ball while dashing towards the boundary.

While sitting down writing a letter, Pringle leaned back in his chair and – ouch! – damaged his back.

Clapped out

A popular player, the West Indian cricketer Clive Lloyd received a great many ovations. His fans were particularly appreciative on the occasion of his last game, which was held at Lord's.

So they clapped, and then clapped some more. And then they stood and turned it into a standing ovation.

Unfortunately, hardly had their hands stopped smarting from the welcome, than they were clapping again, as Lloyd returned to the pavilion – out for a duck.

A wee indiscretion

It is impossible to ignore the call of nature; you just have to go, but not on a cricket pitch, in front of a multitude of spectators.

In 1995 Wayne Radcliffe of the Yorkshire club Newmillerdam fell foul of a ruling made by the Wakefield and District Cricket Union, which banned him for five years for urinating on the pitch. Radcliffe had to plead guilty, but in mitigation he said he had been desperate and, anyway, had turned towards some trees to prevent spectators from witnessing the act and to protect his modesty.

Bare facts

Streakers are so familiar on sports fields these days that spectators barely raise an eyebrow. But a couple of streakers who attempted to get their fifteen seconds of fame during the Asia–Rest of the World game at the Oval rather wished they had thought better of it and stayed fully clothed. Ultimately they were chased and dealt with by what one journalist writing of the incident described as, 'those lovely Oval stewards who are better suited to belonging to the SAS than showing people where to sit'.

Blowing their cover

During the 1996 World Cup between Kenya and Zimbabwe in Lahore, a helicopter was used to dry the pitch with its powerful downdraught after rain had stopped play.

But all it managed to do was to blow the covers away, spilling more water on to the pitch. As a consequence the match was abandoned altogether.

A Case of severe nerves

Somerset's Cecil Case was a bag of nerves after he had been given out 'hit wicket' in a match against Nottinghamshire at Taunton in 1930. He had fallen on the stumps while trying to avoid being hit by a rather lively ball from Bill Voce.

In fact, Case was so nervous that, instead of picking up his bat to take back to the pavilion, he marched back with one of the stumps under his arm.

On Fairway and Green

The game of golf has produced countless amusing moments at the expense of players and spectators alike. From lost balls and wayward caddies to over-zealous fans and baffling bunkers, the life of a golfer is never dull, and often beset by a catalogue of mishaps and mistakes.

Jaws – the game!

In Britain, the only animal you are likely to see as you drive your ball down the fairway is the odd rabbit or squirrel, dog or cat.

It would be a little less comforting to read a sign saying 'Do not feed the alligators', an example of which can be found at the Marriott Hotel golf course in Orlando, Florida.

On the third hole in the third round of the Zimbabwe Open at Harare in 1993, Ben Fouchee and Jurie Visagie, both South Africans, almost had a close encounter of the snappy kind with the course crocodile.

As he crossed a bridge, Visagie nearly trod on the crocodile's tail, which could have had catastrophic results. He finished with an 80 and said he was lucky to be alive. Fouchee finished on 71, but put that down to the fact that the same crocodile went for his wife, who was caddying for him, leaving him to concentrate on his shot.

King, Clark and a cow

Cows eat grass and the odd bramble, sometimes even the odd nettle, but gutta-percha?

It happened in 1963 as S. C. King played R. W. Clark on the tenth hole at Guernsey. Clark had hit his shot into the rough, and while looking for his ball, he found that a cow was eating it.

The pair played the course again the next day, but they were keeping a close eye out for bovine intruders. This time it was King whose ball landed in the rough, while Clark's was safe on the fairway.

Remembering the cow incident, Clark put his hat over the ball, and went off into the rough to help his opponent to find his wayward shot. But when he returned to the fairway the cow was there again, and this time she had eaten his hat.

Making a breast of it

In 1994 Tony Jacklin was trying to get out of a bunker on the thirteenth hole during a British Seniors event. In his attempt to lift the ball clear of the bunker, it rebounded on to his chest.

Unaware that there was a penalty for this type of incident, he put the wrong score on his card. As a result he was disqualified.

Not to be sniffed at

In February 1994, Colin Montgomerie shot a 76 in the first round of the Hong Kong Open. It was his worst competition performance for a year, and he put it down to a smell.

He was allergic to garlic and onions, and a horticultural preparation that was being sprayed around the golf course to keep the grass healthy was very reminiscent of what is, to some, an extremely appetizing odour. But it was not at all pleasant for Montgomerie, and made him feel quite nauseous.

Off the ball

Missing the hole is one thing, but missing the ball is another matter entirely. It does happen, as Hale Irwin proved in the third round of the 1983 Open at Royal Birkdale.

He had left his putt no more than a couple of centimetres from the whole on the par-3 fourteenth, and must have taken his eyes off the ball as he went to tap it in, for he missed the ball completely.

He incurred a one-stroke penalty, which cost him the match. He ended up as joint second, one stroke behind the winner, Tom Watson.

One too many

The Welsh golfer Ian Woosnam managed to lose £218,334 in winnings, and all because he was carrying one club too many.

At the 2001 Open at Royal Lytham and St Anne's, Woosnam was docked two strokes for carrying fifteen clubs instead of fourteen. He had just birdied the first and had gone back into the joint lead, when his caddie, Miles Byrne, told him that he was carrying an extra driver. Woosnam finished the tournament joint third, four strokes behind the winner, David Duval, but without the two-stroke penalty he would have been runner-up, and considerably richer.

Photo finish

If victory in a major championship is virtually assured, a golfer would doubtless have no objections to seeing the press there to record his outstanding achievement. In 1937 Harold McSpaden did not share this view, however, when Densmore Shute retained his US PGA title as a result of McSpaden's bad luck.

McSpaden had a 1.2-metre (4-foot) putt for victory at the last hole, but the snapping photographers disturbed his concentration. He missed the putt and lost the first extra hole.

Presidential problems (1)

Presidents Bill Clinton, George Bush Sr and Gerald Ford were enjoying a game of golf in the Bob Hope Invitation Tournament at Indian Wells in California when, on the first hole, Bush sent a spirited drive right between the eyes of a San Diego woman, shattering her glasses. She was given first aid and taken to the Eisenhower Medical Center for ten stitches.

Later on, Bush still had another target to hit: on the fourteenth he pelted a spectator on the buttock.

Ford caused similar spectator damage during the tournament: while playing the seventeenth he hit a woman on the finger, drawing blood.

Presidential problems (2)

For the President of the United States of America, all kinds of precautions must be taken when entering public areas to do things that ordinary people like to do. In this instance, in 1996, it was a game of golf.

Secret-service agents were in place; marksmen were in the bushes; the course had been checked, as had the clubhouse staff; the men's locker room had been cleared; bags were scanned. But President Bill Clinton had left behind his golf shoes, and no replacements could be found. He shot 84.

Putt it down to bad luck

Waiting for the inevitable to happen is not always advisable. South Africa's Denis Watson fell foul of this attitude in the 1985 US Open. He missed out on the title, and all because he waited too long for his putt to fall into the hole.

He was at the eighth hole during the first round at Oakland Hills, and the ball came to rest on the lip of the cup. He didn't tap it in. Instead, he waited, hoping gravity would eventually bring its influence to bear on the recalcitrant spheroid, and ease it into the hole.

It did – eventually. But by then Watson had exceeded the time allowed for waiting for a putt to enter the hole.

He was cursing himself three days later, when he learned that his 72-hole score put him just one stroke behind the winner, Andy North.

Snakes alive!

The moral of this tale is, be careful when you reprimand your caddie, because his reaction may be rather extreme. This might have been the case at the 1985 South African Masters, where Vaughan Tucker gave a caddie a ticking off because he had moved the player's ball without permission.

But the caddie was not happy to be spoken to so harshly, and disappeared into the rough for a while, returning a moment later waving a snake at the terrified Tucker.

The rights and ... er, lefts of golf

Left-handed golfers must ensure they have left-handed clubs, one would assume, but this was not the case for a golfer who featured in a story in 1898, which appeared in the magazine *The Golfer*.

He had a full set of left-handed clubs on a seaside course open to the public, not far from Edinburgh, but the odd thing was, he was right-handed.

Much to the surprise of the onlookers, he attacked the ball at the first tee in grand style with his left-handed club, but hit the ball with the back of the club. Thus did he complete the course. The magazine reported that, when asked how he got on, he replied, 'Very well, seeing it was my first game.'

Waters lands in his namesake

Alan Waters was a professional at Worplesdon Golf Club in Surrey, and had accepted a lift on the golf cart of the club captain, Alec Justice, during a mix-foursomes contest.

Waters was just a little startled when the cart seemed to take on a life of its own, veered off line and dumped him unceremoniously into the water at the Pond Hole.

Wrong pate, mate!

It is possible to slip up in sport merely by having one's hair too short, it seems.

In March 2002, the Liverpool and District Alliance told an amateur golfer, Tony Jackson, that his close-cropped pate was not acceptable. Jackson, a former Lancashire champion, had his hair cropped about a year before the haughty letter arrived from his club treasurer Bill Yates. He maintained that the shorter style was necessary when he was playing in hot climates, and anyway, he usually wore a baseball cap when playing, so his hairstyle was not an issue.

His excuses were not good enough for Mr Yates, though. Such things as extreme hairstyles and earrings were 'more usually associated with municipal golf rather than the venues where we like to play', according to the letter.

Jackson was unrepentant: 'I'm a county player and I've always upheld the standards and etiquette of the game. Whatever happens I'm not going to change my hairstyle – in any case, I always wear a baseball cap when I'm playing.'

In considering what the Alliance would do if Tiger Woods turned up to play with short hair, he mused, 'Would they ban him, too?'

Yates told the *Daily Mail* that Jackson was not banned, but needed merely to talk to officials about the situation. 'I know it's hard on the boy,' he told the paper 'but who's going to set the standards? Several years ago we lost a lot of top venues due to the behaviour and appearance of some of our members. Two other members with short hairstyles have been allowed to play because they have accepted our guidance.'

A most expensive putt

When is a piece of sand not a piece of sand? When it's a piece of grass, of course, and it loses you the Open.

At St Andrews in 1970, Doug Sanders needed to cover about 30 feet to beat the great Jack Nicklaus. He had to do it in two putts, but his first left him 30 inches short of the hole.

'I was confident, standing over it, and then I saw what I thought was a little piece of sand on my line,' Sanders told reporters afterwards. 'Without moving my feet, I bent down to pick it up, but it was a piece of grass. I didn't take time to move away and get reorganized. I mishit the ball and pushed it to the right of the hole. It was the most expensive missed putt in the history of the game.'

The following day he lost the eighteen-hole play-off to Nicklaus by a single stroke.

Cooper's blooper

Henry Cooper, better known as a boxer than a golfer, was nonetheless fond of a round or two of golf.

On one occasion his trousers split, right in the wrong place. 'I didn't have a clue what to do,' Cooper told reporters. 'But about thirty women around the green rushed forward offering safety pins.'

Having a ball – or not

To lose one ball may be regarded as a misfortune. To lose seven looks like carelessness. But Sweden's Anders Forsbrand managed to do it after taking ninety-three shots for seventeen holes in the 1994 French Open at the National course in Paris. He ran out of balls on the eighteenth.

He had lost five in water and another pair had gone into some deep rough.

Having a splashing time

Generally, it is nice to have fans, and Gary Player must have thought so too when he came off the eighteenth green at the Congressional Country Club after a practice round in 1976.

Finding himself besieged by autograph hunters, Player reached for his pen. But the fans were so eager that they pushed him into a lake.

A wee question of priorities

The moral of this story is, when caddying in an important match, make sure you visit the loo before stepping out on to the course.

The American caddie Chuck Hoersch did not, and it cost his boss, Sophie Gustafson, the £110,000 first prize in the WPGA International match at Gleneagles in 2001.

Gustafson was playing Laura Davies in the semi-finals, and finished all square. But in the following play-off, Hoersch decided he could not wait any longer, and nipped to the portaloo. Then, to catch up with the action, he used a buggy.

However, the rules state that caddies as well as players must walk, not ride, and so Gustafson was disqualified. But for the fact that Gustafson is his girlfriend, Hoersch may well have found himself an ex-employee after such a costly mistake.

Crazy golf

Golfing etiquette was all but forgotten in a game in 1993 at Sabal Palm Golf Club in Florida. Two players, Howard Polley and John Tennyson, were aggrieved by the fact that another player, Hugo Torres, and his fellows were too slow.

To show their contempt, Tennyson and Polley played the seventh without even nodding to Torres and his party, or in any way acknowledging their presence. Their behaviour upset Torres to such an extent that an argument developed and Torres hit Tennyson across the back with his pitching wedge, while Polley then took a swing at Torres. At this point Torres's arm got in the way, and the club broke. In spite of the pain he was suffering, Torres summoned up enough energy to stab Polley in the neck with the broken shaft of his own club, and Tennyson and Polley ended up in hospital. Torres was obliged to pay a visit to the local jail, where he was released on $10,000 bail.

They never did finish their game.

Horns of a dilemma

During a game between Otway Hayes of South Africa and John Panton of the United Kingdom at Houghton Golf Club in Johannesburg in 1951, a woman golfer wearing a bright red sweater became the focus of some very unwanted attention.

There was a scream. The players looked up to see a bull in full charge, horns lowered, heading towards the hapless damsel in distress. Fortunately, she was quick-witted enough first to hide behind a tree, and then to don a mackintosh to cover the offending sweater. The bull, no longer able to see the rage-making stimulus, just sauntered off.

Dark deed

Sports injuries are all part of the job, an occupational hazard, they come with the territory. But sustaining a more mundane injury away from the sportsfield is somewhat less acceptable.

During the Ryder Cup in the United States in 1971, the American Billy Casper had to miss the singles match because of a broken toe. He had damaged the digit while groping around in his St Louis hotel in the dark, trying to find his bedroom.

Bunkered!

Within the context of golf, being rescued from the bunker usually means getting your ball out and back on to the fairway. Not so for D. J. Bayley MacArthur, playing at Rose Bay, New South Wales, in 1931.

His ball landed in a dreaded bunker and naturally he went in to retrieve it, but in seconds he found himself up to his armpits in sand, so heavy had been the rain.

The 89-kilogram (14-stone) MacArthur shouted for help which, thankfully, arrived.

Caught with his pants up

If he had not been at such pains to keep his trousers clean, Craig Stadler might have been joint second in the 1987 San Diego Open at Torrey Pines. He had hit a shot that had gone underneath a bush, and the position of the ball was so awkward that it was necessary for Stadler to kneel to get to it.

He was rather too fond of his trousers, though, and to muddy them by kneeling was more than he could stand. So he knelt on a small towel that his caddie used to clean his golf balls. This was strictly against the rules, however, because it constituted 'building a stance'. His misdemeanour had not passed unnoticed, either, because the match was televised, and some viewers phoned in the following day. As a result, Stadler was disqualified for not having included the penalty in the score he had signed for the previous day.

Aiming for the cup (1)

Golf balls land in strange places, but Hale Irwin, taking part in a 1973 United States tour event, did not expect his to land where it did – within the bra of a spectator.

Fortunately, he was spared the embarrassment of removing

the ball from its resting place with the club of his choice; instead he allowed the woman to remove it herself.

Aiming for the cup (2)

Great Britain's Leonard Crawley may not have been aiming for the cup exactly, but the result was the same. It was during the 1932 Walker Cup match at Brooklyn, and Crawley's wayward drive to the eighteenth managed to hit the treasured trophy, on display outside the clubhouse, giving a severe dent.

Thrills On Wheels

There's nothing quite like the noise and the smell of the race track. Exhaust fumes fill the air as the whine of engines provides the incidental music to one of the most thrilling sports on earth. However, this high-powered sport is certainly not without its tales of craziness, stupidity and downright doziness.

The wrong formula

Some people, it seems, are fated not to make it. Bobby Unser was a legend in the Indie 500. He had won it on three occasions – 1968, 1975 and 1981 – but, when he attempted to compete in Formula One with BRM, luck was not on his side.

In 1968, the year he first won the Indie, he wanted to race in the Italian Grand Prix, but a prior commitment in the United States caused him to pull out. Then, at Watkins Glen, New York, he crashed a car while practising, and managed to blow a couple of engines, too. So he took a different car for the race itself, but had to retire with engine failure, and it proved to be his one and only attempt at Formula One racing.

Hop in, love

The British driver Tony Fall had stopped his Lancia to wait for the correct time at the final control in the 1969 Portuguese TAP Rally, and was greeted by his wife.

As the crowd surged forward, the police asked if he could drive on towards the control. Obligingly, Fall told his wife to jump aboard while he moved the car the 10 metres or so to reach the control. Technically, though, he was carrying an unauthorized passenger when he was crossing the finishing line, and was duly disqualified.

Seconds away

Poor George Grinton did not appreciate the difference between minutes and seconds when, during the 1925 sidecar Tourist Trophy on the Isle of Man, he got a signal from the pit saying '3'.

Grinton mistakenly believed he was three minutes ahead of the rest of the field. He decided to slow down a little, to avoid taking unnecessary risks, believing himself to be in an unassailable position. As two cars suddenly came into view, and raced past him at high speed, he soon realized that the signal actually meant three seconds, not three minutes.

Sure enough, a somewhat crestfallen Grinton ended up third.

Vintage comedy

They had to let the train take the strain back in 1896 on the occasion of the first London-to-Brighton Rally.

Only fourteen out of the thirty entrants reached Brighton by road. During the run, a Bollée tricycle managed to nip through a hedge and was towed out by a cart. Another machine turned turtle, and ended up – complete with occupants – in a pond.

And others that were unable to make it under their own steam had to be taken to the south coast by train.

The chequered rag

For some inexplicable and rather infuriating reason, Rudolf Caracciola's leading Mercedes began to slow down quite dramatically as he neared the finish in the 1937 British Grand Prix at Donington.

The cause of his failure to cross the line first became apparent when, having finished third, he looked over his car and found that an oily rag had been left by one of his mechanics in the supercharger.

My giddy ant(eater)

Imagining the many different types of obstacles that could get in one's way is a racing driver's nightmare; hitting any sort of object at such high speed can be damaging and devastating, and change the course of a race.

During the 1963 East African Safari Rally, Swedish driver Erik Carlsson was leading the event in his Saab when he hit an anteater.

Putting his foot under it

Track marshals managed to hamper the progress of René Arnoux when his Ferrari stopped with an electrical fault.

On the occasion of the 1983 South African Grand Prix at Kyalami, Arnoux was in the middle of a qualifying session. His car stationary, he asked the marshals if they could push it to a safer place. They did – but went over Arnoux's foot, leaving it badly swollen for the race.

When technology is the pits

Formula One engineers had no idea what they had created when they developed new technology that enabled them to use computers to tweak cars electronically – and from a distance.

While the high-tech equipment took away the time-wasting necessity of pit stops, the change to the rules that allowed the new technology – called bi-directional telemetry – also meant that hackers could sabotage cars while they were on the track.

The chief operations engineer for the Williams team, Sam Michael, told reporters in 2002, 'There's potential that, if your system's not coded properly, you could have a situation where it gets false messages. If it happened, the biggest danger you would have is a change on the engine side – detonating the engine.'

For the technically minded, the idea is that the data is assessed and engineers can then tell whether they need to make any changes to key areas in the car's system, such as traction control, power, fuel and oil consumption, and differential. The pit can then warn the driver of any changes via a steering-wheel display, and he can press a button to acknowledge.

But Gilles Flaire, a team technician and a former French secret service agent, told *Sport Auto Moto* magazine, 'If the bi-directional telemetry allows those in the pits to control essential parameters of the car, it will be possible to interfere in the systems through devious methods.'

Back and forth to victory

André Boillot had to cross the line twice in order to win the 1919 Targa Florio road race in Sicily in his Peugeot.

He had already left the road no fewer than seven times, but the last was when he crashed into the grandstand just a few metres from the finish line. Because this last crash had caused him to spin rather violently, he crossed the line backwards. Since this would have meant a disqualification, the car was manhandled and turned round so that it once again faced the right way, and was driven across the line a second time.

Size does count

Nigel Mansell had been signed up for McLaren for just two months, but had to withdraw from the opening two races of the 1995 Formula One World Championship because the cockpit in the McLaren Mercedes was too small. He had to be replaced by Mark Blundell, who slotted into the cockpit cosily.

Size counted in a different way when Peter Harper's Sunbeam Tiger was disqualified from the Coupe des Alpes in 1966. He had an exhaust that was too small. Not too large, which would have given him an advantage, but too small, which could not have given him any extra power.

Fall guy

While waving to the crowd after finishing fourth in the 500cc US Motor Cycle Championship in 1989, Kevin Magee fell off his bike and broke his leg.

As you were

Louis Chrion of France had been taking part in the Monte Carlo Rally during the 1920s when he found himself, and his car, in a ditch. It took hours for him to get the car out of the ditch and back on the road, only to be shunted back into the ditch by another competitor.

On his head be it

Mika Hakkinen's team boss, Ron Dennis, was not too pleased with his driver when Hakkinen drove out of the McLaren garage to get to the starting grid for the 1999 Australian Grand Prix in Melbourne.

Hakkinen was unaware that his air line was still attached to his car, which pulled down a gantry – right on to Ron Dennis's head.

Dastardly and Muttley, eat your hearts out!

Winning is all, and some people will go to extraordinary lengths to achieve victory, which is what happened during the 1902 Paris–Vienna road race.

For Charles Jarrott, driving a Panhard, the trouble began when, on the second day, the car's wooden chassis collapsed as it approached the overnight stop at Bregenz. Jarrott, though, was determined not to let a few pieces of wood get in the way of success. All that was needed was some way to strengthen the frame, and they could at least make it to the end of the next stage, which was at Salzburg.

Still pondering on the problem of how to repair the chassis, Jarrott and his trusty mechanic George Du Cros retired for the night at their hotel in Bregenz. Then Jarrott had an idea, which he explained later: 'I was just getting into bed and had turned to put out the light, when my eye fell upon a stand used for carrying a tray,' he said. 'And in a second I perceived that the four legs of that stand were exactly what I wanted.'

It was a bit late to ask the proprietor if they could buy the stand, so they decided to take it and answer questions later.

Then came le deuxième problème: how to drill holes in these suddenly priceless pieces of wood, to accommodate the bolts. Du Cros suggested it would be a good idea to drill against the wall in order to get better purchase. Jarrott was to recall, 'He was delightfully successful, but the trouble was that he drove it through too far and brought down half the plaster. And then, in endeavouring to show how easy it was on another portion of the wall, he succeeded in bringing that down, also.'

But their problems did not end there, as Jarrott managed to bore a hole in his arm and, in an effort to staunch the bleeding, ripped up bed sheets to use as a bandage.

Jarrott recalled, 'There was nothing in the room we did not utilize for something or other. I hate to think what must have been the expression on the proprietor's face when he discovered what had taken place.'

The next problem was how to get the pieces of wood out of the hotel without being discovered. The solution they reached was to put them down their trouser legs.

This is what they did, and they managed to repair the vehicle and get it back on the road. They eventually reached Salzburg and carried on towards Vienna. Problems were still arising at every turn for, at one point, Du Cros had to lie on the bonnet and hold a towel against the pipe to keep the water in the radiator.

Less than four miles from Vienna, the Panhard's gearbox broke. Jarrott 'borrowed' a bicycle and rode for help. But Du Cros could not just sit idle so, while Jarrott was away, he managed to obtain help from a horse-drawn cab. When Jarrott got back, he saw the car being towed behind the cab to the finishing line, and was aghast.

An indignant Jarrott cut the tow rope and got behind the Panhard's wheel, managing to guide the spluttering car across the finish line. And the engine finally went phutt-phutt, and died.

Fire and water

For reasons unknown, no one told Franco Cortese that his treasured Alfa Romeo had gone up in flames on the eve of the 1933 Mille Miglia. An electric spark had ignited some petrol fumes, and the car was no more than a burned-out shell.

Cortese only discovered the distressing situation four hours before the start. Immediately he set about overseeing the rebuilding of the car and, with just an hour to go before the start, all had gone well and Cortese looked like he had a functional car in which to race. However, one of the mechanics had contrived to pour water, instead of petrol, into the fuel tank, which then had to be removed and cleaned out.

Cortese was late for the start of the race and, although he expected to win, he came in second.

Twenty-one years later in the same race, just after the start, Giuseppe Farina hit a tree while trying to avoid a spectator who had strayed on to the road. Farina, in a Ferrari, was out of racing for two months after suffering a broken arm.

In 1957, the same race witnessed a spectacular crash after the French daredevil Jean Behra decided to do some last-minute practice before the race. He was hospitalized after his Maserati had crashed into a lorry.

Back in 1932, an unfortunate collision took place between Nazio Nuvolari's Ferrari Alfa Romeo and a tree. Nuvolari's co-driver was Gianbattista Guidotti, who was given quite a fright by men in cloaks. When he came round at the side of the road, he could not see Nuvolari, but realized he was on a stretcher that was being carried by four men wearing what he thought were Ku Klux Klan robes. So he shut his eyes and pretended to be dead.

Fortunately, the mysterious figures were just monks from a local order, who traditionally helped drivers injured in the Mille Miglia. They were merely taking him to their monastery hospital for treatment.

Crew cut

Raymond Joss had no time to lose during the 1963 Monte Carlo Rally. He and his crew of three were on the Chartreuse special stage, when the Rover three-litre car went off the road.

Two crew members got out to push the car back on the road but, impatient to get going again, he sped off, leaving one of his crew in the road. He had been unable to get back into the car in time. The hapless crew member went to drink some wine with locals in a bakery and watch as the other competitors sped by.

Ultimately, Joss's impatience proved to be his downfall, for crossing the line without a full complement of crew, he was disqualified.

Snow fun

Spectators can often be a liability when a rally championship is at stake.

During Stage 3 of the Monte Carlo Rally in 1994, the even leader Armin Schwarz and second-placed Colin McRae both skidded on snow thrown by spectators, and left the road. Schwarz ended up in overall seventh place, while McRae was tenth.

In the 1968 Monte Carlo Rally, drunken spectators threw snow on to the road during a tricky mountain section, while Gerard Larrousse was vying for the lead in a works Renault Alpine.

Information that is the pits

It was the final hour of the 1935 Le Mans 24-Hour Race when René-Louis Dreyfus's Alfa Romeo caught up with a Lagonda, believed to be the leading car, which looked to be in a rather bad state, having had to make several stops due to oil-pressure problems.

So when Dreyfus's pit colleagues said he had passed the leading car, he felt quite pleased with himself; so pleased, in fact, that he decided to take it easy.

It transpired that Dreyfus's colleagues had given him the wrong information, as he had not, after all, passed the Lagonda when he decided to slow right down and imagine he was taking a leisurely Sunday drive.

Crossing the line, he fully expected that winner's honours awaited him, but of course they did not. To the poor man's surprise, he was actually five minutes behind.

Rock-solid opposition

The Swedish racing driver Bjorn Waldegaard was taking part in the 1979 Monte Carlo Rally, but found that the Villars stage had been blocked by rocks, put there by spectators.

Waldegaard's co-driver had to get out and lever the rocks away, but the Escort was denied seventy-five crucial seconds – and ultimately victory in the rally. The Lancia Stratos of Bernard Darniche of France won by just six seconds.

And the winner is ... and the winner is ... and ...

The Austrian Alpine Rally of 1974 is most notable for having three winners. Such was the confusion that, in the end, officials threw up their hands and erased the whole sorry mess from the motorsport calendar.

Achim Warmbold's BMW had the smallest number of penalty points. But the organizers disqualified him because he had approached a control from the wrong direction. However, the driver argued that the control had been in the wrong place and that the Renault team manager had blocked the route at one point, deliberately.

With Warmbold ruled out, another winner was declared.

This was Bernard Darniche, driving a Renault Alpine. He was just one second ahead of Per Eklund, who was driving a Saab. The Saab team were not happy about this at all. The regulations, they said, stated that timing was to be to the whole second, but organizers had announced that the stage times would be timed to one-tenth of a second. Saab argued that, if the tenths were ignored, Eklund would have won by a second.

Long after the rally had ended and the motorsport season had moved on, these disputes were still being thrashed out until, in a blaze of bewilderment, officials decided it would be better if the race had never happened.

So it was dropped from the calendar, after expunging the results of the 1974 fixture.

A pushover

It looked good for Jack Brabham in the 1959 Formula One World Drivers' Championship until, at the United States Grand Prix at Sebring, the last race of the season, he ran out of fuel with about a mile to go.

Despite the slip-up, the result was not too disastrous. Brabham coasted for a while, and as he came to the second-to-last corner his teammate Bruce McLaren, who had been in second place, caught up with the Australian and slowed down, but Brabham waved him on. If he offered any help, he could be disqualified.

Brabham was determined not to lose. Once the car had finished its coasting about 500 yards from the finish, Brabham got out and started to push. And he pushed, and pushed, and pushed some more.

By the time he reached the finish – with the crowds going wild with excitement – he dropped to the ground through sheer exhaustion. But he had come in fourth, and the points he had secured were enough for him to win the championship title.

The Sport of Kings

A day at the races is the ideal way to spend a summer afternoon for many. A drink in the bar, a flutter placed with one of the track bookmakers, the atmosphere, the anticipation, the excitement when a favoured horse is coming into the final furlong neck and neck with the favourite.

As with most sports, though, things can go wrong, whether through horse, jockey or trainer error. We have galloped through a number of amusing stories to bring you a colourful selection, including a couple of tales from the dog-racing world.

Dead cert
Dying in the saddle can be an awful slip-up. It happened though, in 1923, when Frank Hayes rode Sweet Kiss – a 20–1 shot – to win a steeplechase at Belmont Park at Elmont, New York.

Over the finish went horse and rider, and friends and connections went in to congratulate him, only to find him dead and slumped in the saddle.

It is the only time a dead jockey has won a race.

Event could have gone to the dogs

Here is a potential sporting slip-up that was deftly avoided. There could have been enormous embarrassment for the Irish Greyhound Racing Board following a suggestion that Viagra could enhance the dogs' prowess on the track, and provide more exciting entertainment for the spectators.

After giving the matter a little more careful thought, however, officials realized that use of the powerful sex-enhancing drug might just result in the wrong type of entertainment. They decided there was no solid evidence that Viagra could possibly enhance racing performance, so in a complete about-turn, they banned it.

Off course

Marker dolls had not been placed correctly on the course during the Prince of Wales Novices' Chase at Chepstow in December 1987. The result was that the entire field took the wrong course, and crashed through a rail on to the hurdles course.

However, the racecourse executive at Chepstow paid out a share of the prize money to the owners of the twelve horses that had been wrongly diverted to a different course.

Mob rule

Wherever large groups of people have gathered en masse, crowds have always had the potential to cause trouble over the centuries.

At the October Derby race meeting in 1776, the leading horse was racing comfortably until an irresponsible spectator decided to influence the course of the race. A report on the first day of that meeting states: 'Just before he came in at the winning post, being crossed by a gentleman on horseback, the rider was thrown; but his leg hanging in the stirrup, the horse carried his weight in, and won miraculously without hurting his jockey.' On this occasion, despite the best efforts of the eighteenth-century hooligan, the outcome of the race had not been affected.

Nearly forty years later, at the 1815 Derby, the Epsom crowd were not too pleased with the jockey, one J. Jackson. He had been beaten into second place on the 7–2 favourite, Raphael, and it can only be assumed that many of the crowd had got good money on Jackson and his horse, for they dragged the poor man from Raphael and set about him.

Jumped back in – and out again

Chris Warren was looking forward to getting back into his stride as a jump jockey after being out of racing for five weeks owing to a broken collarbone. His comeback was arranged for November 1988, when he would be riding Allied Force in a novices hurdle race at Newbury.

On the day, however, he discovered his car had been stolen during the night. When he eventually found the vehicle, it had been badly vandalized. Fortunately, the riding gear he had stored inside the car, ready for his big race, was still intact, so he managed to get a lift and made it to Newbury just in time.

As it turned out, Allied Force was not a force to be reckoned with on that day, and fell at the first fence. Warren fell, too, and the same collarbone was broken once again.

Unstable stable

After the poor performance that his horse, Wickham, displayed during the 1910 Grand National, Frank Bibby, Wickham's trainer, was angry and disappointed after what was a quite promising start.

There were twenty-five runners, and almost half of them

were soon out of the race, but Bibby's three – Wickham at 66–1 and the two stable-mates, Caubeen and Glenside – were still in contention, and this was where Wickham's unruly behaviour began. Having collided with Caubeen, sending the horse and its mount on to the turf, he ran across Glenside at a fence, bringing down himself and the other horse. Thus, thanks to Wickham, all three runners from the same stable were eliminated. The winner that year was Jenkinstown.

Bibby did score well in the following year's National, however, as Glenside won the race at 20–1.

Weighty problem

Before the race in the Netherkelly Notices' Chase, Richard Rowe had left the paddock at the correct weight, but at the weigh-in after the race he was 14 pounds (6.3 kilos) lighter. As a result of Rowe's sudden weight loss, his horse, Hogmanay, was disqualified from first place in the chase, held in November 1988.

Puzzlingly, after studying film of the race, stewards just could not pinpoint where on the course the lead weights that had been attached to the saddle had become detached.

The question of the missing stone was never resolved.

Horseradish, anyone?

Security was perhaps not as tight in the nineteenth century as it is now. How else could a group of picnickers find themselves still sitting beneath the rail of the first fence with an entire field of racehorses thundering in their direction?

In 1871, this unlikely scenario occurred. Oblivious to the fact that a race had begun, the picnickers picnicked on and it was not until the horses were dangerously close that the group realized what was happening, and ran away from the scene without further delay.

Horses and hound

It was a horse race, but a dog came a rather creditable fourth in the Tote Each Way Handicap Hurdle at Lingfield in December 1985.

The greyhound, a racer itself, slipped its owner's lead and decided to join the race. It was all too much for its owner, Vi Cowan, though. She collapsed and had to be revived.

Marathon mutt

Mental's Only Hope was the name of a greyhound who set a new record with his sporting slip-up at Wimbledon Stadium in March 1961.

Dissatisfied with the usual sprint, Mental's Only Hope decided to turn it into a marathon, and just kept running, dodging the owners and trainers and other officials who were trying, without success, to catch him. He eventually slowed up and stopped out of sheer exhaustion, having run for a total of 30 minutes and 29 seconds.

Out to grass – voluntarily

On the day of the 1952 Goodwood Cup, Aquino II was at 2–1, and tipped to do well in the race. Unfortunately, Aquino II was a horse very much prone to lapses of concentration, and had been fitted with blinkers to ensure he was focused on the track ahead, and avoiding the distraction of the fields on either side. Success in the race did not bode well from the start, though, as Aquino II first tried to turn around and go back to the paddock. His jockey managed to get him back on course, but the animal had only galloped for a furlong (201 metres) before swerving into the centre of the course.

Finally, when Aquino II reached a bend coming off the straight, the blinkers proved useless when the horse espied lush grass, adorned with buttercups and daisies. He waited until he saw a gap in the railings, and as soon as one came up, the horse sauntered into the field and partook of a verdant feast, oblivious to the outcome of the race.

They're off. Not!
In 1863 during the Derby, a total of thirty-four false starts were recorded. Many of them had been caused by the rank outsider, Tambour Major, and it was to the eventual relief of many that he was finally left behind.

The favourite in this race was being ridden by George Fordham, but he was beaten by a neck. On his way back to the unsaddling enclosure, Fordham overheard a spectator say that he had thrown the race. Nicknamed 'the Demon', Fordham did not appreciate such an aspersion on his character, so he promptly leaped off his mount, took hold of the hapless punter and threw him into a bed of nettles.

Whacked and fagged out!
A bright hopeful called Young Whack was disqualified by the Dublin Turf Club in July 2001 after he failed a drugs test at Navan in Ireland, but the seven-year-old had never been near any stimulants.

It transpired that the drug Young Whack had been 'taking' was nicotine. His trainer, Noel Meade, could offer no clue as to how Young Whack had got a sniff of the tobacco. The stewards accepted that Meade had 'taken all reasonable precautions', but poor old Young Whack had to be disqualified nonetheless.

'He'll be some horse when we get him off the fags,' Meade quipped.

Slip Up slipped ahead

It was an aptly named horse that won the Devon and Exeter in 1986 – Slip Up!

Roger Charlton was riding towards the post on Amantiss and was just a few metres from the line. Suddenly, Amantiss decided to drop him on to the grass.

Amantiss was first past the post but, without its jockey, it could not be officially placed. Taking advantage of his rival's mishap, Slip Up slipped in from second place to first, and won the race.

Travel sickness

All White was a rank outsider in the 1919 Grand National. His usual rider, Robert Chadwick, was out of the race through injury, and so another jockey, T. Williams, was brought in as a substitute rider.

He needed to reduce his weight to the required level of 9 stone and 10 pounds (just under 62 kilos), and so set about fasting for several days before the ride.

However, on the day of the race, he decided to have a plate or two of cockles and mussels from a seafood stall at Aintree, but that proved to be a costly error for Mr Williams.

After a jump on the second circuit, Williams was forced to halt his mount and lean over to be violently sick. He recovered and set off again to catch up with the rest, but eventually had to settle for fifth place.

Unstable boy

It was a stable lad who made the sporting slip-up that caused a favourite to win the Grand National in 1898. Manifesto could have got a hat-trick, had the boy not been so careless.

Before this race, the horse – which had won the 1897 race, and would go on to win the National in 1899 – had been sold for £4,000 to Mr J. G. Bulteel, and he had put it in the charge of a new trainer. However, the stable lad left open the door, and Manifesto went walkabout, trying to jump a gate during his wanderings.

After he was found it was discovered he had bruised his fetlock, and had to miss the race as a result.

The stable boy is said to have made himself scarce, and was never seen again after realizing his unfortunate error.

Shocking fall

When Aly Branford was found twitching after falling from his horse during a National Hunt race at Wye, ambulance staff were mystified. He had been thrown over the running rail, and his twitching could not be fathomed, until his rescuers found he had landed on an electric fence used to keep sheep from roaming.

Not a safe bet

The British politician and well-known horse-owner, Horatio Bottomly, thought he was on to a good thing when he devised a 'foolproof' way of winning on the horses, but it was to cost him – not win him – a fortune.

Before a race to be held at Blankenberghe in Belgium, Bottomly purchased all six horses that had been entered and hired six English jockeys to ride them. The riders were told exactly the order they were to pass the winning post. Then, so as to leave nothing to chance, Bottomly backed all the horses.

Halfway through the race a thick sea mist descended on the proceedings, and the entire course was engulfed by it. As a result, no one could see anyone else, least of all the jockeys. Horses were unable to see where they were going, and the judges could not see the horses. If any did finish the race, it was more by accident than skilful riding. And so Bottomly lost out in grand fashion.

As a complete aside, Horatio Bottomly once called at the home of Lord Cholmondeley, whose surname, as everyone knows, is pronounced 'Chumley'. Bottomly, known to be somewhat impish, asked the servant who answered the door if 'Lord Chol-mond-ley' was at home, giving the consonants their full value.

'It's pronounced "Chumley", sir,' came the somewhat starchy reply.

'Very well,' said our Horatio, 'then tell him Horatio Bumley is here to see him.'

Tell us a Knother one!

Mick Morrissey left the starting gate on a horse called Knother, but passed the post on Royal Student. The horse was not renamed halfway round the track, of course, as Morrissey actually began the race on one horse and ended it on another.

This extraordinary event happened during the two-mile steeplechase race at Southwell in 1953. At the fifth fence, Royal Student fell, not only throwing his rider off but creating an obstacle for Knother, who crashed into him, throwing Morrissey out of the saddle. Morissey went high into the air, but landed squarely in the other horse's saddle, and it was Royal Student, and not Knother, that took him to the end of the race.

What's up, Duc?

It is hard to tell which jockey has been parted from his mount the highest number of times, but the Duc of Alburquerque must be up there with the winners – or losers, depending on how one looks at it.

He made racing history in 1963 when he was given 66–1 against finishing the Grand National while still actually in the saddle.

The Spanish aristocrat seemed to divide his time between the saddle and the stretcher, beginning the race but not usually ending it, and finding himself, instead, in the Royal Liverpool Infirmary.

He almost broke his neck in 1952, when he fell at the sixth fence, and in 1963 it was at the fourth fence that he and his horse parted company. His horse collapsed in 1965, and his stirrup broke in 1973, although he managed to cling on for eight fences before coming off.

He fell off during training in 1974, but rode with a broken collarbone and his leg in plaster.

Bang off target

Sally Oliver was looking forward to her day trip to Bangor. The Midlands trainer had a horse running there, and it came in first. However, when the stewards required her attendance for the purpose of an enquiry, she was nowhere to be found. She was in Bangor, they were in Bangor, but it soon became apparent that they were in different Bangors. Bangor-on-Dee was a small village in Shropshire, where the race was being held. Bangor in North Wales, about a hundred miles away, was where Sally had journeyed, believing the race was to be held there.

Neigh, lad!

On the occasion of the New Stand Design Team Slaney Novice Hurdle at Naas in Ireland in January 1999, Paul Carberry made a mistake that cost him not only the race, but landed him with a ten-day suspension.

He thought there was another lap to go, but he was wrong. He was riding along comfortably on Sallie's Girl, and was making no attempt to increase his pace. When he saw other horses picking up the pace at speed, he kept back tucked in behind Glazeaway, ridden by Conor O'Dwyer.

Carberry even called to O'Dwyer that there was another lap left, but O'Dwyer, wisely, chose not to take any notice. It was only when Carberry and Sallie's Girl crossed the finish line that he realized his terrible mistake.

Evening meal

Inkerman's patience was wearing thin, and he was growing tired of carrying his rider round a track. And so, in the 1863 Grand National, the horse dumped its rider and wandered off at the Canal Turn.

The horse's connections spent hours looking for the errant equine, and eventually found him, late at night, some miles away from the track at Aintree, munching grass in a field.

The napper and the nap

When Graham Bradley was struck down with tiredness on 18 May 1994, the date of a race at Worcester, he decided to have a nap in his car. He overslept, however, making him late for the race, so stewards fined him £100.

In the event, Macedonas, the horse he should have ridden, went on to win the Handley Castle Novices' Chase, ridden by Simon McNeill, the jockey who replaced Bradley.

Bradley told reporters afterwards, 'I was here an hour and a half before racing and I had a doze in the car. When I woke up, I was a minute too late to weigh out.'

The National that never was

On 3 April 1993, the 150th Aintree Martell Grand National went down in history as the race that never was, following a fiasco with the starting tape.

The race had already been disrupted when a number of demonstrators had to be removed from the first fence, but when the horses had settled, and the starter, Captain Keith Brown, called the riders into line and start the race, the strong wind caused the starting tape to become caught around one of the horses, resulting in a false start being called.

After the horses returned, settled and lined up again, another false start was called as some of the horses had been too near the tape when it lifted; Richard Dunwoody had become entwined in the tape on the back of Won't Be Gone Long. Though nine horses had pulled up before the first fence, most of the field had already set off at pace, and did not realize a false start had been signalled.

Race officials attempted to attract the attention of the riders as they reached The Chair, but were mistaken for protesters, following the earlier problems on the racecourse.

Though seven horses finished the four and a half mile race, with Esha Ness ridden by John White crossing the line first, the race was later declared void, costing the UK Treasury and betting industry millions of pounds.

Blood, Mud and Machismo

Ever since William Webb Ellis invented the game of rugby, the sport has thrilled spectators all over the world. And none more so than in the nations associated with it: England, Wales, Ireland, France, Scotland, Australia, New Zealand, South Africa ...

A game of hulking men, lots of spills, rough and tough scrums, kicking, running, and passing an oval ball about the field, with its fair share of blood, mud and machismo.

It has its lighter moments, of course, as the next few entries wholeheartedly prove.

Unrepeatable event

Not a tale to make a Welshman feel proud, but the consolation is that this incident did happen a long time ago.

Back in 1881 at Blackheath, England and Wales turned up for a rugby union international, but Wales had arrived in London two players short; the men's invitations had gone astray. So two university players were quickly recruited, but failed to muster the quality of the missing players, even though they both had Welsh qualifications.

It appears that the Welsh side was so humiliated by the circumstances that the fixture at Blacheath was never repeated.

Laughing Boy

Rugby is usually taken so seriously by its fans and players, so on the occasion of South Africa's visit to New Zealand, to take on the All Blacks in 1937, the sight of a grown man giggling like a naughty schoolboy was a rare thing to behold.

The Springboks' player Boy Louw had suffered a blow to the head that had resulted in a bout of concussion, and so he barely knew where he was for the rest of the match. Disorientation apart, he found himself unable to stop giggling; most unheard of on a rugby pitch.

During one of his fits of laughter, Louw broke off from the game and asked his captain, Danie Craven, what was happening and what he ought to be doing. Craven suggested he should try to stop the All Blacks' prop, Dalton, from coming through the lineout.

So, at the next lineout, Boy charged into Dalton while the referee was looking the other way, giggling as he did so and looking to his captain for approval.

The Springboks did manage to win the match 13–6, however, in spite of laughing Boy's unpredictable, yet amusing, behaviour.

Nice try!

While playing for Kukris against Panaga, Dick Dover scooped up a loose ball as he broke away from the scrum, dashed 75 yards with it and touched down for a try. Thinking it strange that no one had challenged him en route, he realized he had placed the ball under the posts of his own team, having become disorientated while in the scrum and run the wrong way...

Own goal (posts)

When one's rugby union club is told to leave its ground to make way for a league club, the response will never be well-received. It happened to Bridgend RFC in South Wales when they were told they would have to leave their Brewery Field home in 1948. They had the last laugh, however, after creeping on to the field under cover of darkness and stealing the goalposts.

Stick-in-the-mud rescue

Rugby pitches can become veritable quagmires sometimes. None less so than during the match between Taranaki of New Zealand and the British Lions in 1977.

When Dave Loveridge of Taranaki sustained a bad knee injury, the stretcher, the usual means of taking a player off for first aid, was deemed inappropriate, and an ambulance was called for.

As a result of the horrendous conditions underfoot, the vehicle got well and truly stuck in the mud, and it was eighteen minutes before both players and spectators could free the wheels and get the vehicle on its way with the injured player snug inside.

No ball!

In 1966, the Colwyn Bay rugby team went to North Wales to play their rivals Porthmadog. The field was set, the crowd waited in breathless anticipation, the teams lined up opposite each other, the touch judges were in place, the referee was ready for the kick-off, the ball was... Despite all efforts to find a ball, not one could be found, and so the match had to be abandoned.

Sock it to 'em, John

When John Roberts turned up to play for Cardiff Athletic against Chepstow in 1937, he had a vital piece of kit missing – his boots.

However, Roberts had set his heart on playing and retaining his place in the Cardiff first team. So he played in just his socks.

Such lip!

Peter Harvey was a scrum-half for Canterbury, New Zealand, and had been chosen to play in an All Blacks tour of Britain in 1905.

He was unable to fulfil his obligation to the famous national side, however, because the prime minister of New Zealand refused to allow him to leave the country. The reason was that he was the only qualified lip reader in the islands.

Light entertainment

Strange though it sounds, some sports fixtures were actually floodlit in the nineteenth century.

In a match between the Scottish Borders towns of Hawick and Melrose on a snowy night in 1879, some 5,000 spectators gathered to watch one of the earliest lit games. Not surprisingly, lighting was not as sophisticated then as it is now, and lighting outside the ground was clearly inadequate to stop a number of people sneaking in without paying.

As soon as the match ended, perhaps to save electricity or to punish the gatecrashers, officials turned out the lights, leaving fans to fumble about and crawl over one another to get out of the stadium; not only in darkness, but in snowy slush, too.

Not settling the score

At Twickenham in 1933, England were playing Wales – always a clash that generates patriotic pride. A kick at the goal by Vivian Jenkins went 'at least a yard outside the right-hand post', according to the *Daily Telegraph*. But the Welsh touch judge raised his flag to show he thought the ball had passed between the posts. The English touch judge did not agree, however.

The result was that the scoreboard carried the wrong score for the rest of the match. Spectators thought Wales had won 9–3 when they had in fact won only 7–3.

Ripping yarn

During scrums and the general rough and tumble of a competitive rugby match, players' shorts are occasionally very badly ripped. When this happens, the usual procedure is for a ring of players to form a circle around the player with the ruined shorts so he can change into a fresh pair.

Not so for the Australian captain Trevor Allen when his side were playing at Twickenham against England during the 1947–48 tour.

He threw convention to the wind, whipped off the damaged garment and walked to an attendant several metres away to get a new pair of shorts, jockstrap on full view, in front of a crowd that included a royal party.

As one would expect, there were those who like to create a

fuss over such things, and there were mutterings within the world of rugby union for some time.

Streak of bad luck

In the 1970s there was a TV documentary that recorded the achievements of a rugby team from Doncaster in South Yorkshire. During its history, the side came bottom of its league more times than any other club, and lost forty games on the trot.

On one occasion the players failed to recognize their own strip because they were covered in mud, and began to tackle their own side.

The entire team was put up for sale in 1980.

Word play

Fly-halfs usually pay very close attention to the game and play an important role in the proceedings, but when Mick English was playing for Ireland against England in 1958, his opposite number Phil Horrocks-Taylor managed to run past him and score a try to clinch the match for the English.

His teammates asked him what had happened, and he replied, 'Well the Horrocks went one way and the Taylor went the other, and I was left holding the hyphen.'

Late arrivals

Mombasa Rugby Football Club boarded a plane in 1974 and flew 475 miles to Uganda for their annual needle match with Nairobi Harlequins. What they were unaware of was that several thousand feet below them, travelling in the opposite direction, were a fleet of cars bound for Mombasa.

Each team, once it had arrived, rang the other to find out where it had got to, to discover the unfortunate mix-up.

Putting the boot in (his shorts)

Sid Going was an All Blacks half-back who, playing for North Auckland, claimed some of the credit for his side's 35-point win over Buller, to win New Zealand's Ranfurly Shield.

The going for Going was good in the 1972 match, and the Buller lads were clearly affected by this man's amazing skill. During a tackle, however, Going lost a boot, and a Buller lock, Orlando Nahr, slipped it into his shorts while no one was looking.

Since no one knew where the missing boot was, Going had to play the rest of the game wearing only one boot.

The luck of the Irish!

Ireland had embarked on a centenary tour of New Zealand in 1975, and had arranged to drop by to play a game against Fiji en route.

Unfortunately, the Fijians were not at home when the Irish team landed – they had left the country to begin a tour of Australia.

The (bad) luck of the draw

While making the draw for the 1995 World Cup, the procedure had to be carried out three times.

The first draw, made in January 1993, did not please Australia and New Zealand, because they said teams from the same pool should not meet again until the final.

The officials agreed, and a second draw was made. But then there was a printing error, which meant that teams from the same pool would still meet before the final.

Eventually, at the third attempt, the draw was made successfully to the satisfaction of all concerned.

Troubled waters

Scotland's W. A. Allan was appointed to referee the Ireland–New Zealand international in Dublin in 1935, but had not reckoned on the Irish Sea slowing him down.

He set off in good time or so he thought, but encountered some rather lively weather, and was still stranded at sea when the match kicked off. So a substitute referee was sent on – R. W. Jeffares, son of the secretary of the Irish Rugby Football Union.

Water music

Rain was certainly instrumental in stopping play of a different kind at St Helen's in Swansea in 1903. It was the start of the Wales–England international in January, and the rain managed to insinuate itself into the instruments of the brass band.

So no play – of the musical variety – was possible.

!#**#@}% , ref!

Newton Abbott player Denys Dobson was a pleasant fellow, really, but he had an unfortunate habit of being sent off, which was a shame, because he had already earned six caps as an England forward.

The reason for his numerous dismissals was owing to his consistent use of obscene language directed at the referee.

Dobson received an eight-month suspension for one such display during a British Lions tour of Australia and New Zealand in 1904.

Compared with the treatment meted out to a referee in Peru, however, Dobson's behaviour was positively saintly. Felipe Compinez awarded a penalty during a local cup competition but, when the goal was scored, angry fans of the other team stormed the pitch and stoned Compinez to death.

Printer's devil

A slip-up of an editorial kind appeared in the matchday programme for an Ireland–France international in 1980, when the surname of the Irish back Colm Tucker was found to begin with an 'F' instead of a 'T'.

Slipped disc

It was the day of the draw for the first round of the 1923–24 Rugby League Challenge Cup competition. Teams were drawn using cardboard discs.

All went well until the draw was almost over. When the officials drawing the balls got to Salford, it seemed that they would be at home to no one, for there was no disc left in the bag for the away team. Strangely, thirty-two discs had been placed in the bag and yet only thirty-one had been drawn out.

Not only was the Salford team mystified, but so was Hunslet, because their name had yet to be drawn.

Eventually, it emerged that the disc with Hunslet's name on it had slipped out earlier in the draw, having become stuck to the back of Swinton's disc, and gone unnoticed by officials.

The League decided to give Hunslet the away tie with Salford, since it was the only possible pairing left. Hunslet did not agree with the idea, but were denied a re-draw.

Aye, aye – anyone eyed my eye?

The 14-stone (89-kilogram) forward Steve Bush, playing for Silverhill Colliery, Nottinghamshire, managed to lose his glass eye during a game of rugby.

Silverhill were playing Daw Mill Colliery of Warwickshire in the 1993 Coal Board Cup, and the game had to be held up for a while after Bush had been spotted looking for something after a hard scrum.

When the referee, Peter Llewellyn, asked him what he had lost, Bush replied, 'My eye.' At first Llewellyn thought that a hospital visit was required, but Bush reassured him it was just his glass eye.

In spite of much searching through the grass, the glass eye, which had probably been stamped into the ground during the scrum, could not be found, and so Bush had to play with an empty socket for the rest of the match.

Whether or not it was down to the fact that Bush was turning a blind eye, Silverhill lost 17–8.

Early bath – then play again

Referees have been known to blow the whistle at the wrong time, but are usually only ever out by a few seconds or the odd minute. When East Midlands were playing Barbarians at Northampton in 1921, however, the referee's watch proved to be far less than accurate.

Adrian Stoop, a former England international player, blew the whistle for the end of the play fourteen minutes early.

Whatever the reason for the players' early bath, they were ordered out on to the field again to complete the game.

Adding insult to injury

An incident during the third round of the Rugby League Challenge Cup tie between Swinton and Castleford during the 1927–28 season led to a change in the rules.

One of the Swinton players had been hurt and was being treated off the pitch, so Castleford thought they could take advantage of having one man more. At one point, Castleford's side, en masse, swamped the Swinton line and it looked as if they were about to score a try.

They were thwarted, however, when a player emerged from nowhere and executed a perfect tackle, preventing the try. Castleford players, robbed of this golden opportunity, could only look around in bewilderment at where the mysterious tackler had come from.

It was the injured player. He had seen the danger, decided he had to act quickly, fought the pain, ran on to the pitch and made the tackle. The Castleford team was outraged, and protested loudly, but judgment was against them. They even went on to lose the match.

Eventually, the rules were changed to state that injured players need to be given permission to return to the field.

Getting carried away

Rugby is a game that produces many injuries, but France's Jean-Pierre Salut must have set something of a record, for he was carried off before he even got on the pitch.

He was about to take part in an 1969 international against Scotland in Paris, and was running up the stairs from the dressing room ready to make his entry onto the pitch.

But he fell and broke his ankle, and was stretchered away.

And now a word from our sponsor ...

It could happen only in America. John Reardon was refereeing a match between England and Mid-West at Cleveland, Ohio, in June 1982, when suddenly the match stopped dead, on Reardon's orders.

The English players wondered what on earth was happening, when Reardon told them he had been instructed to stop play because a local TV station was covering the fixture, and at this point they had to show advertisements.

Torn between making money from advertising revenue and ensuring that TV viewers did not miss vital play, the TV company had done a deal to have the game stopped whenever the ads were due to be broadcast.

Cap that!

Arnold Alcock, who played for Guy's Hospital, could be excused for wondering why he was so special when he was sent an invitation to play for England at Rugby. The great event that would earn him his first and only cap was a match against South Africa in 1906.

The reason Alcock received his call-up paper, however, was due to a clerical error. The invitation should have gone to Lancelot Slocock, who played for Liverpool.

Alcock's big game proved to be his only international outing, as he was completely out of his depth. Slocock, on the other hand, played for his country eight times.

Celebratory trickle

Great Britain won the inaugural Rugby League World Cup, held in France in 1954. And, of course, a celebration was called for.

Naturally, the trophy, which was presented by the French Rugby League, was filled with champagne, but it leaked. The cup had not been made watertight where the handles joined the bowl.

Couldn't bank on it

It was a proud day for Frank Clayton in 1884. He had been selected for the first New Zealand tour to Australia.

At the bank where he worked, his bosses would not believe him when he told them of his selection and they refused to give him the time off.

Drunk and incapable

Corby rugby team were on a tour of northern England in 1989. After a heavy night on the town the previous day, they staggered manfully on to the field of play to take on Whitby.

The referee soon realized that most of the Corby side were too drunk to play and so he abandoned the match. To clear up any doubt on the matter of their sobriety, the scoreline of 80-0 provided ample proof.

No butts!

As Christians are a traditionally peace-loving people it was a surprise when, during a JPS Trophy match between Runcorn Highfield Rugby League Club and Wigan in 1989, a born-again Christian named Bill Ashurst was sent off for head-butting eleven minutes after taking the field.

Forty-one-year-old Bill was one of nine amateurs playing for Runcorn Highfield, the team somewhat depleted due to a players' strike. He was also their coach, and was one of the substitutes, but came on in the second half, only to take an early bath.

Sorry, mate, you'll have to pay

As the referee of an important match, it is most unusual to be charged an admission fee to enter the ground, but Cyril Gadney found himself in this awkward situation on the day of the 1936 international between Wales and Ireland at Cardiff.

As time went by, and the match was nearing kick-off, officials began to worry why the English referee was nowhere to be seen. They waited a while longer and were wondering what contingency plans they might make, when Gadney was seen queuing up to get in, and having to pay for the privilege.

He had arrived at the ground in good time and told the gateman he was the referee, but the gateman refused to believe him, thinking it was a likely story, made up to gain free entry to the ground.

So it was that Gadney had to queue with the spectators, much to the embarrassment of Cardiff's stadium officials.

Another try

In 1901 the governor of New Zealand, Lord Ranfurly, offered a trophy to the New Zealand Rugby Union. The handsome shield was commissioned from England, and would have been accepted as a much treasured gift until someone noticed that, on the engraving, the shape of the ball was round instead of oval. And the goalposts were for football, not for rugby.

The unfortunate engravers were told to try again, and get it right this time.

I'm off, by George!

It was all too overwhelming for George Crawford, as he refereed Bristol's match against Newport in September 1985.

The clash soon deteriorated into a mass brawl, and Crawford could neither control it nor put up with it. So he walked off, and a local official had to take his place for the rest of the game.

In need of air

The United States of America were playing their first rugby union international match since defeating France in the final of the 1924 Olympic Games in Paris.

But the Americans, taking on Australia in Los Angeles, had made some fundamental errors. The pitch was neither long enough, nor wide enough. Furthermore, it was not marked properly. The ball felt like a soggy balloon and was badly in need of inflation. Eventually, after an announcement over the PA, a pump was produced, the ball was properly inflated and the match got under way.

Despite the earlier slip-ups, the Australians remained focused, and achieved a 24-12 victory.

Time out

Referee John Cail was rather embarrassed when he officiated in New Zealand's match against Yorkshire during the Maoris' tour of Britain in 1888–89, because his watch had ceased to function, and so he had to go into the crowd and borrow one.

Putting the Boot In

Football is fast, furious, fantastic, and extremely tribal. Some would say it is the best spectator sport as adrenaline pumps through the body while chants are chanted, anthems sung, scarves waved. Nothing excites the sporting public quite like football, and we seem to cry out for more and more of it as television viewers.

Football is also a serious money-making business, with record transfer fees and players' salaries growing ever more. It's not all serious, though, as there are many hilarious stories concerning players, referees and spectators alike whose embarrassing stories have taken up thousands of column inches in local and national newspapers.

Mismatch

In 1973, a Wolverhampton Sunday League team, Oxbarn Social Club, arranged a friendly match in Germany, reasoning that it would be a good chance to have a holiday and hone their playing skills at the same time.

They were expecting to play on a recreation ground, so it was not until they arrived at their opponents' luxury stadium that they realized they had arranged a match with a top German side. SVW Mainz, a first-division team, were expecting to play Wolverhampton Wanderers, who were at the time one of Britain's top teams.

The Oxbarn club's secretary told journalists at the time, 'I thought it looked posh, and when I heard the other side were on an eight-pound bonus to win, I said to myself, "Something's wrong." '

The Oxbarn goalkeeper was seen to fall to his knees, as if praying for the match to end, after the fifteenth ball had sailed past him and into the net. The final score was SVW Mainz 21 Oxbarn Social Club 0, but the British side was glad of the practice.

Rio felt not too grand

Injuries can happen when they are least expected – not always on the field.

In the case of the world's most expensive defender, Rio Ferdinand, of Leeds United and England, he managed to strain a tendon in his knee. He was not playing at the time, but was sitting in front of the television with his feet up.

His manager, David O'Leary, explained to reporters, 'It was a freak accident, and typical of this season. It wasn't even on the training ground. He was watching television and had his foot up on the coffee table. He had it there in a certain position for a number of hours ... and strained a tendon behind his knee.'

Unlucky for some

The number thirteen has long been regarded as an unlucky number by the superstitious. It proved to be so in another way for the match between Leicester City and Stockport County in May 1921, which managed a crowd of just thirteen.

The explanation for the lack of support was that both teams were playing away from home, because Stockport's ground had been temporarily closed. The match was held, instead, at Old Trafford, the home of Manchester United.

Netted

Chick Brodie was goalkeeper for Brentford in the late 1960s, and on one occasion was playing in an away game at Lincoln City in the Fourth Division.

He was responding to a high cross and thought it would be a good idea to stop the ball from going into the top of the goal by hanging on to the crossbar. However, with an ear-splitting crack, the crossbar snapped and down came Brodie, ensuring that he and two defenders got tangled up in the netting.

The match had to be suspended for forty-five minutes while repairs were carried out. Perhaps not helped by Brodie's unconventional goalkeeping, Brentford went on to lose 2–0.

Window of opportunity

According to the *Sun* newspaper in February 2002, it is vital for Norwich City that a window cleaner's sponge is present at the ground on match days, because without it they cannot win.

The Canaries had won on twelve occasions in the 2001–2002 season when window cleaner, Keith Adams, had cleaned windows there, but when he was somewhere else, the team could only draw four matches and lose one.

It is fortunate that Adams's boss is a Norwich fan, for he ensures that the window cleaner is always at the ground on match days.

Franc exchange

At the beginning of a 1950 club match in France, one of the captains accidentally swallowed the five-franc piece that was being used to decide which team played at which end first.

Not the real McCoy for Real Madrid

When a group of Everton stewards made a presentation of a bronze statuette to Real Madrid, officials there thought it was a miniature version of the statue of the footballing legend Dixie Dean, which stands outside Goodison Park, but it was not.

Real Madrid officials were so moved by the gesture that they said they would put the statuette in their trophy cabinet, alongside figures of their own soccer greats, but not only did the small figure have the wrong hairstyle (not at all like Dean's combed-back style), it was also taller and slimmer, whereas Dean was stocky.

The bronze's kit was more modern, too, and it was dribbling a lightweight ball, whereas Dean wore a 1920s jersey in the rugby style, and played with a heavier ball.

Who it really was, no one knew. A spokesman for the British

club said the stewards had made a 'genuine mistake'. They had wanted to take something special to Real Madrid, but the Spanish officials had mistakenly thought the statuette was of Dean.

'There are some names in football that transcend all barriers of time and geography and Dixie Dean is one of them,' said the spokesman in early 2002. 'His name is known at Real and they were touched enough to put him in their trophy cabinet. To be honest, they could come here and present us with a statue of one of their greats like Stefano and we probably wouldn't know if it looked like him. The important thing is that it was a presentation from Everton FC and a symbol of friendship.'

You're out of line

When a team named Over Wallop Reserves played a side representing a local pub called the Lardicake, the match was far from dull when a replacement referee was needed for the match in the Andover and District Sunday League. As a qualified referee, Over Wallop's manager, Terry Gilligan, agreed to officiate.

During the game, the linesman, Phil Cooper, was rather aggrieved when Gilligan ignored his flag for a foul and signalled for the match to continue. When Gilligan did eventually stop play, it was to order Cooper off the pitch for behaviour most unsuitable for a linesman. Cooper refused to go, so Gilligan abandoned the match with his own side leading 1–0. Cooper was eventually fined by the Hampshire FA and suffered a ninety-one-day suspension.

Damaged goods

It is always a joy to receive a cup after winning a coveted title or a competition, but sometimes joy can turn to overexcitement. In the case of Charlton manager, Jimmy Seed, whose team won the

1947 FA Cup final, he accidentally dropped the gleaming trophy, damaging the lid.

The cup was due to be paraded at a civic reception, so emergency repairs had to be carried out quickly at a local garage.

Twenty-four years later, it was Liverpool's reserve team coach, Phil Thompson, who damaged the lid of the FA Cup. He left his team's London hotel after the final, and managed to drop the lid, damaging it so badly that it would not fit back on the cup itself.

Pick a card, any card

It is rare for a football match to turn into a card game, but in a match between River and Oeiras in the State League of Piaui, north-east Brazil, in early 2002, Paulo Araujo was 'carded' five times by the referee Edmilson Timoteo da Silva.

Araujo's 'hand' consisted of two yellows (for two separate fouls), followed by a red, which sent him off the pitch. Another yellow followed because he had remained on the pitch, unbeknown to the referee, who had not spotted him until he needed to give him a second yellow card for a foul. The final red card followed automatically.

The official reason why the referee had not realized that Paulo was still on the field was because he thought that many players looked alike.

'I consider this a serious mistake,' announced Edson Rezende, president of refereeing within CBF, the Brazilian Football Confederation.

The referee said, 'I've never seen anything like it. People even said I'm going to get a place at the Guinness Book [of Records] for the amount of cards I gave.'

Seeing red

Melvin Sylvester was a football referee, and a good one by all accounts. He knew the rules, and as far as he was concerned, the only penalty for someone caught punching a player was an immediate sending-off.

In April 1998, forty-two-year-old Sylvester was overseeing an Andover and District Sunday League match between the Southampton Arms and Hurstbourne Tarrant British Legion. He had stepped in when the official referee was taken ill. In a moment of sheer madness, however, he lost his temper and threw a punch at one of the players, and had no choice but to send himself off.

Sylvester had reacted a little too hastily to what he thought was a push by a Hurstbourne player, saying he was 'sorely provoked'.

'I punched him after he had pushed me from behind,' said Sylvester. 'He then swore. I just couldn't take any more. I blew my top.'

So he gave himself a red card and a spectator substituted for him for the rest of the match.

Not the final whistle, then

There were just seconds left until the end of the match when Arsenal played Blackpool at Highbury in 1955. Arsenal were winning 4–0 and their left-back, Dennis Evans, heard a whistle.

Thinking it was the referee, Frank Coultas, blowing for the end of the game, Evans casually flicked the ball into his own net. His goalkeeper had also assumed that he had heard the final whistle, and began picking up his cap and gloves.

In actual fact, the whistle had been blown by a spectator, so the referee had to award Blackpool a goal.

On me 'ead, Bill

In 1898, during a game between Sheffield United and Liverpool at Anfield, United player Bill 'Fatty' Foulke responded aggressively to the shoulder charge inflicted on him by Liverpool player, George Allan.

Known for his explosive temper, Foulke picked Allan up by the ankles and stood him on his head in the mud, before bouncing him up and down to make his point felt.

A man of two games

It is difficult to combine an interest in two games, especially when torn between football and cricket. But Mickey Stewart found himself in this situation in 1956.

He was on tour at the time in the West Indies with the England cricket side, but wanted to play soccer for Corinthian Casuals in the FA Amateur Cup final. He set off on a 4,500-mile journey from the Caribbean, which took him two and a half days.

Unfortunately for Stewart, he arrived at Wembley too late – just three minutes after kick-off. Not only was he unable to play, but his side also lost 4–1.

Terrain stopped play

Pre-season friendly matches at Reading's Elm Park ground had to be cancelled in 1986 because the groundsman, Gordon Neate, had accidentally sprayed concentrated weedkiller on the pitch instead of a selective solution.

It meant that three-quarters of the playing surface was ruined.

A thirsty game

During a ninety-minute game, footballers naturally get thirsty.

In August 1979, the players in a match between Winthorpe Wanderers and British Seedhouses, held at Newark in Nottinghamshire, decided they wanted a drink. There was a handy container at the side of the pitch, and so they took their fill.

The players should have checked the contents more closely, however, for the container also held Paraquat (a weedkiller) and a corrosive acid the groundsman used for burning holes in the pitch.

Eleven players needed hospital treatment but, fortunately, none of them were seriously hurt. They were mercilessly teased for weeks afterwards, though.

Leg before goal

To score one own goal is unfortunate; to score two own goals seems like carelessness. For Herbie Roberts of Arsenal, the unthinkable happened during a match at Highbury against Derby County in October 1932.

While attacking from the Clock End during the early part of the game, Derby's left-winger, Dally Duncan, sent a hanging ball across the field, and Herbie stuck out his leg. Unfortunately, the ball hit it and went into the net.

After the restart, spectators saw what television viewers decades later would call an instant replay. Duncan centred a ball, and Herbie was there again. In went the ball for a second own goal.

It may have been small compensation for Herbie that the match ended not with disaster for his side, but a more respectable 3–3 draw.

The power of prayer

There have been many odd reasons for failure, but the excuse offered by Senhor Isadore Irandir of the Brazilian side Rio Preto stands alone. He let in a goal after just three seconds of play when his side were up against Corinthians at Bahia Stadium. From the kick-off, the ball went to Roberto Riveline, who drove it with a powerful left foot from the halfway line. It went straight past Senhor Irandir's head.

His excuse was that he was still on his knees in the goalmouth doing his pre-match prayers.

Missed goal

November 1961 was an important time in the history of Morecambe Football Club. They were in the Lancashire Combination League, and defeated Chester, who were in the Fourth Division, 1–0 in the second round of the FA Cup.

Unfortunately for the majority of fans, the goal was scored in the first minute, and all but a handful of fans had seen it. Most fans had travelled to Chester by train, arriving thirteen minutes late at the station. Then they had to catch a bus to get to the ground in time, but their journey was delayed once again when the buses became stuck in traffic jams.

Own goal (1)

During a match against Liverpool in 1960, Charlton winger Sam Lawrie, in a moment of distraction, decided to pass the ball back to his goalkeeper.

The goalkeeper, Reed, was looking the other way at the time, however, and Lawrie had to stand horrified as the ball made its slow and infuriating way into the back of the net.

Own goals (2 and 3)

In just four days, Tommy Wright, an Everton defender, managed to score two own goals, and each came in the first minute of its respective match. He scored one in a Merseyside derby against Liverpool on 4 March, and managed to repeat the feat in an away game against Manchester United.

Absent friends

Brighton's goalkeeper, Perry Digweed, did not appear for his team's match against Bournemouth in the Second Division in September 1988 because no one had told him he was playing.

In similar circumstances the West Bromwich Albion striker Fabian de Freitas was not around when his side played Crewe on Easter Monday 1999, as he thought it was an evening kick-off.

Team-mates and officials tried to contact him by phone, but the line was engaged during a lengthy call held by his girlfriend. West Brom went on to lose the match.

The Gillingham captain Mark Weatherley was prepared to be loyal to his side at all costs when snow drifts looked like preventing him from getting to the game. He trudged six miles to get to the FA Cup tie against Wigan in 1986, and when he arrived at the ground it was only to discover that the match had been called off.

The name's Bond – but don't tell anyone!

Shrewsbury Town's manager John Bond understandably feared for his safety in 1992 when his team played at Burnley. Before his current post, he had had a spell in charge at Turf Moor, and had received threats from Burnley fans, who were not at all impressed with his performance for their beloved club.

So when Shrewsbury played his former club, officials thought he would be safer if he disguised himself as a steward, watching the game from the back of the stand.

Despite the elaborate disguise, Bond's team lost 2-1.

Sprake's progress

Gary Sprake was a talented, if erratic, Welsh international goalkeeper who played for Leeds United. During a 1967 title match against Liverpool at Anfield the ball rolled to Sprake. He was about to throw it wide to Terry Cooper, but Cooper shouted to him, 'No, no!' because he could see an opposing player bearing down on him.

'So,' Sprake said, when looking back on the match many years later, 'I went to pull the ball back to my chest, as I often did, and it just flew over my left shoulder into the net.'

His team-mates were blissfully unaware of their goalkeeper's slip-up, but suddenly heard a cry from the crowd. Sprake was standing on the edge of the 18-yard box with his face in his hands.

The disc jockey selecting the music for half-time played the Des O'Connor ballad, 'Careless Hands'.

Unlucky Star

In the training ground of Red Star Belgrade, fans were so angered by their team's poor performance in their country's premier league that they launched a physical attack on the team.

Red Star, who were defending champions in early 2002, trailed nine points behind their traditional rival, the first-ranking Partizan Belgrade. The fans did not like it at all, so they shouted obscenities and told players they brought shame on the club. Masked assailants then chased players into the locker room and set about them with sticks, causing police to intervene.

One of the club's midfielders, Mihajlo Pjanovic, told journalists, 'Red Star has been in crises, but this is no way to solve problems.'

The fans' behaviour was not dissimilar to that of Lazio's supporters in Rome. Not long before the Belgrade incident, they too confronted players because of their poor performance in the Italian Serie A.

What a mouth!

Alex Stepney, in goal for Manchester United during a match away to Birmingham City in 1975, had a reputation for his vocal strengths on the pitch.

He shouted so enthusiastically and energetically to his team-mates that he had to be taken to hospital with a dislocated jaw.

Hand in glove with the law

How do you turn a sporting slip-up (or was it a goalmouth gaffe?) into a superstition? By leaving your goalkeeper's gloves behind.

When Jack Fairbrother (Newcastle United's goalkeeper when they won the FA Cup in 1951) managed to lose his gloves, he borrowed a pair from an obliging policeman who was patrolling the ground and passing behind the goal.

Newcastle won the match, and Fairbrother decided that, from then on, he would wear policemen's white gloves, and was said to be a frequent visitor to the police station in Market Street.

Colour blind

In the 1930–31 season, a Sheffield team was playing in an annual game against a Glasgow side.

Sheffield's captain, Jimmy Seed, kept passing the ball to the referee, but for a good reason. The referee was wearing a white shirt, and so were Seed's team-mates.

Consequently the referee was persuaded to go to the dressing room and put a stop to the confusion by changing into a dark shirt.

Doppelclanger

Mick Pullen of Bognor Regis Town could be excused for not knowing what was happening when he was sent off for no reason in the 1992–93 season in the Diadora League.

After Mick's twin brother Paul had been involved in a scuffle with opponents, the referee sent Mick off instead. Despite protests of Mick's innocence the referee refused to back down.

As the team's player-manager, Mick was in a good position to dictate matters after the incident. He said, 'Paul thought it was hilarious, but I'll make sure *he* serves the three-match suspension!'

Point taken

The Wheatsheaf pub team from St Helen's, Auckland, in County Durham earned one point by drawing just one match out of the thirty they played during the 1994–95 season. They lost the other twenty-nine games.

Unfortunately they were docked two points because on one occasion they failed to field a team, which meant that they finished the season at the bottom of the league with an improbable 'minus one point'.

The team secretary, Gordon Heseltine, who also played centre-half, told reporters, 'This has to be the worst season in history. I can't remember anyone ever ending up in the red before. It's pretty embarrassing, but at least we know we can't get any worse!'

Bottled-up anger

Fans were far from pleased in March 1969 when Palermo lost a match 3–2 against Napoli.

They decided to vent their anger on the referee and his linesmen by throwing bottles. The referee and the other officials had to be rescued by a police helicopter, before the 5,000 furious fans could cause them any serious damage.

Flag of convenience

Phil Boyce was about to referee a local soccer match in Shrewsbury, when he managed to lock himself in the changing rooms, and become stranded there, wondering what on earth he should do.

It was fortunate for Boyce that he had a linesman's flag to hand. He waved it furiously out of the window until someone saw it, and he was freed from his predicament. The match eventually got under way after a twenty-minute delay.

Two Kevins and an Alf

In 1973, during a World Cup qualifier between England and Poland at Wembley, England desperately needed a goal. Sir Alf Ramsey decided he wanted to send Kevin Hector on to the field as a substitute, and said, 'Kevin, get stripped.'

It was Kevin Keegan, though, who heard the great man's command, and began to remove his tracksuit.

When Ramsey realized his instructions had been misheard, he tried to repeat his original request, but it was too late. By the time Hector did get on to the pitch, there were only ninety seconds of the game to play, so neither Kevin managed to have any effect.

Celebration today, injuries to Morrow

Celebrations can sometimes be more dangerous than the match itself. In the 1993 Littlewood's Cup final between Sheffield Wednesday and Arsenal, Steve Morrow, the Northern Ireland international, scored the winning goal.

With a sense of elation, a jubilant Tony Adams hoisted Morrow into the air, but then dropped him. Morrow suffered a broken shoulder.

A spell of mayhem

An allegation of witchcraft arose when a Nairobi goalkeeper threw a cap into his goal. It was 1973, during a match between Abaluhya and Hakati. The Abaluhya side thought that the cap that the Hakati goalkeeper had thrown to the back of the net represented a spell, and would make the Hakati goal impenetrable. They alleged that an old coin, some crushed herbs, a needle, some animal skin, some roots and leaves were sewn into the band of the cap – an effective combination.

About halfway through the match, one of the Abaluhya players ran into the Hakati goal and snatched the cap, running with it to the touchline. He was chased by the entire Hakati team. The result was chaos, and the match was abandoned.

Witch way to sporting success

In April 2002, the repayment of a ten-year-old debt was finally promised to witch doctors who were thought to have put a hex on the Ivory Coast football team.

The witch doctors, from a village called Akradio, were called to help the team to victory at the 1992 African Nations Cup, but claimed not to have been properly rewarded for their skills. It was then believed that they had put a jinx on the team as punishment, as over a ten-year period the Ivory Coast achieved nothing in the African Nations Cup.

After the Ivory Coast team had performed badly in the 2000 African Nations Cup, they were sent to a military camp as a punishment and forced to frogmarch and go to lectures on patriotism. In the 2002 finals in Mali, the team were knocked out again in the first round.

As a last resort, in an effort to placate the Akradio witch doctors, the Ivory Coast's defence and civil protection minister, Moise Lida Kouassi, promised the village a bottle of spirits and the equivalent of £1,400 during a visit to the village in April 2002.

Meanwhile, in Chile, a bottom-of-the-table team, Deportes Arica, employed a witch in early 2002 to help them to escape relegation to the second division. They hired Eliana Merino to cast out 'evil spirits' from the dressing room, the stadium and the players' kit.

The ritual involved candles and smoke to 'purify' the team before kick-off. One of the team's defenders, Marcelo Muñoz, said, 'When you're at the bottom of the table, you'll do anything to improve your position.'

In 2002 the bishop of Oxford agreed to exorcise a football stadium to try to lift a 'gypsy's curse'. Oxford United's chaplain called in the Right Reverend Richard Harries after the team's poor run of results.

A moose, a-loose

Football players often collide with one another on the field, both in matches and in training.

The former Norwegian international defender, Svein Grondalen, was involved in a collision with a difference when out on an early-morning jog with a friend, when he injured himself colliding with a moose.

Becks backs a loser

At his 26th-birthday photocall in 2001, David Beckham made a huge mistake when he wore a hooded top with a picture of a face on it. Unbeknown to him, he was sporting a picture of Adolf Eichmann, the Nazi official responsible for the murder of millions of Jews.

Becks vowed he would never wear the top – sent to him by a US fan – again after the photocall at his in-laws' home in Hertfordshire.

Blowin' in the wind

It was a windy day when Newcastle United had begun checking into their hotel ready for their match at Brighton in November 1989. They were taking kit from the team coach when a gust of wind got behind the trolley containing the pile of kit baskets, and sent it hurtling down the prom. Coming the other way was a Number 67 bus, and shorts, shirts and jockstraps went flying.

United beat Brighton 3–0, further alienating the local populace.

Can we have our ball back, please?

Wolverhampton Wanderers' Peter Knowles was in a celebratory mood after a goal against Portsmouth at Fratton Park. In his excitement he gave the ball a hefty kick and sent it out of the ground.

It was never found, and because Portsmouth were so short of money at the time, they sent him a bill for a new one.

Stamp of disapproval (1)

Even the world of philately is not immune from slip-ups of a sporting kind. In Norway, the postal service printed 1.3 million stamps bearing a picture of the wrong man.

The stamp commemorated the National Soccer Federation's centenary and was supposed to show Lars Johan Hammer, a twenty-seven-year-old referee, but the man on the stamp bore no resemblance to Hammer whatsoever.

It was not until the end of March 2002, that the man on the stamp was identified as a German referee, Peter Hertel, from SG Borussia Fuerstenwalde in Brandenburg, who presided over the Junior Norwegian Cup in 1997 alongside Hammer.

Hammer was philosophical about it. 'I don't have glasses or a beard,' he said, 'and I must say I was stunned to see this strange referee on the stamps.'

A spokeswoman for the postal service, Elisabeth Gjoelme, said the incident was embarrassing. 'When we bought the photo it was in good faith that it was the right one,' she said.

Before Hertel was identified, the postal service launched a campaign, including a veritable wanted poster in the Oslo-based Verdens Gang, Norway's largest newspaper, to discover the identity of the impostor.

The stamp was issued, complete with the wrong image, in April 2002.

Stamp of disapproval (2)

In 2002, stamps issued in the small European republic of San Marino were printed with the wrong scores to celebrate Italian footballing victories.

According to the stamps, Italy beat Czechoslovakia 4–2 to win the 1934 World Cup in Rome, but the correct score was 2–1.

Furthermore the stamps state that Italy beat Hungary 1–0 in

the 1938 World Cup Final in Paris, when they actually won 4–2. There were six stamps in the set issued in the run-up to the World Cup and, when the error was discovered in early 2002, the postal service said they were working to release a new set, with the correct scores.

Deciding shot

It was a single goal that settled a 1968 match in the Third Division between Plymouth Argyle and Barrow, but it was scored by the referee.

There were just ten minutes to go, and Barrow were awarded a corner kick. The ball was kicked by a Plymouth defender, but intercepted by Barrow's George McLean, who took a shot, but it was wide; so wide, in fact, that it sailed towards the referee who was standing 11 metres from the goalmouth.

In all fairness, the referee saw the ball coming and tried to get out of the way, but it bounced off his foot and went into the goal.

The referee had no choice but to award the goal to Barrow.

Don't publish – and be damned

Back in 1936, the Football League was not a supporter of the pools companies, believing that they introduced a disreputable element into the game. In an effort to try and hamper the pools' companies business, they refused to publish fixtures. Posters for forthcoming matches would therefore advertise 'Manchester United versus ?'

Not only did this policy confuse the fans, but also the clubs. Some did not arrive at matches, while others went to the wrong grounds.

Somehow, the pools companies managed without the correct information, discovered who was playing whom and the lists were complete and correct.

Eventually, the League and the pools companies became allies, after the League changed its policy.

A match of two games

In 1885 Arbroath beat their opponents by a massive 36–0, but they did have an advantage, because the opposition was the wrong team from the wrong game: they were cricketers.

Arbroath had mistakenly invited Orion Cricket Club to play a game of football, instead of Orion FC of Aberdeen.

The cricket club sportingly made the effort, despite having neither football strip nor boots, and seemed to enjoy the game, even if fate had bowled them a googly.

Climb to victory

Millwall were leading 1–0 against Walsall in November 1948, when their goalkeeper, Malcolm Finlayson, suffered a head injury and was taken to a local hospital. After a check-up he was told he would be all right to go back in goal.

When Finlayson and a Millwall director returned to the

ground, however, they found that all the entrances were locked and there was no way of getting in unless they climbed the perimeter wall, which is just what they did.

Finlayson returned to the game when Millwall were 3–1 down, but helped his team to a surprising recovery, winning 6–5.

Mean sheen

It is a poor workman who blames his tools, but in the 1927 FA Cup Final, the goalkeeper managed to blame his jersey.

The deciding shot of the match came from Cardiff's Hugh Ferguson, but it managed to slip through the arms of the Arsenal goalkeeper, Dan Lewis, a Welsh international. Officials decided that the new jersey Lewis was wearing still had its sheen, and in future all new goalkeepers' jerseys had to be softened in the wash before anyone was allowed to wear them on a match day.

Back out

After missing a good chance against Aberdeen in March 1991, Rangers striker, Mo Johnston, was so angry with himself that he picked up a lump of mud and threw it down in sheer frustration. In demonstrating such aggression, however, he managed to put his back out, and ruled himself out of the next match.

Bum deal
England had just beaten Tunisia 2–0 in the 1998 World Cup, and the first goalscorer Alan Shearer and the England coach Glenn Hoddle were being interviewed on television.

For some reason, only Hoddle was in shot, while Shearer's words were heard off camera. The reason for the unusual angle was that Shearer was standing in front of a huge banner reading MARSEILLES, of which the last five letters were off shot, and the first letter was hidden by Shearer's head. Showing great professionalism, the cameraman had chosen to spare Shearer's blushes.

Pitch battle
Arbroath may well have won their match against Rangers 4-3 at home in their 1884 match, but there was little to celebrate, due to a battle over the size of the pitch.

The Glasgow club objected that it was too narrow and, when the tape measures came out, officials found it was 35 inches (90 centimetres) short. So there had to be a replay, and Arbroath lost 8–0.

A bad example
In September 1995, when Dave Lucas knocked a fellow referee, Peter Wall, unconscious, the skirmish led Lucas to be banned from football for five years.

There had been a mix-up and both referees had turned up to oversee an under-elevens' match between two Birmingham teams.

During an argument over who should referee the match, Wall received the unexpected blow to the head, but did officiate after receiving treatment.

A spokesman for Birmingham County Football Association

told reporters, 'There are regular cases of players or managers assaulting referees but, as far as I'm aware, it's unprecedented for a ref to hit another ref.'

Catch a falling jar ...

Dave Beasant, the England goalkeeper, was ruled out of action for the first few weeks of the 1993–94 season during his time at Southampton. He had dropped a jar of salad cream on his big toe. As the jar began its rapid descent to the floor, he tried to catch it with his foot, but in doing so he severed a tendon.

Beasant was out of action for two months.

Down and out

In the inaugural World Cup in 1930, the United States team trainer was not a happy man following a disputed Argentine goal.

He was still inwardly seething when he dashed on to the pitch to attend to a hurt player. As he threw his bag on the ground, he broke a bottle of chloroform and anaesthetized himself, and had to be carried off on a stretcher by his team.

The USA lost the match 6–1.

Making a fist of it

Injured Denis Law had to sit out Manchester United's 1968 European Cup semi-final with Real Madrid because of injury. When Bill Foulkes scored for United, Law punched the air in delight, forgetting about the low ceiling on the dugout.

His fist went through the plaster, and he was injured for even longer while he nursed a broken bone in his hand.

Spectator sport

Northwich Victoria were only able to field eight players for a GM Vauxhall Conference match against Maidstone United in November 1986. So Northwich's chairman Derek Nuttall addressed the crowd over the PA system to ask whether any of the 738 spectators wanted to play.

To Nuttall's amazement, three volunteers came forward – Mark Fogg, Steve Garnett and Rick Parkin.

As Northwich were in a fix, they could not be choosy about whom they sent onto the field, they failed to find out that one of the three volunteers had consumed a pork pie and a couple of pints of beer before arriving at the game.

Despite their handicap, Northwich still managed a 1–1 draw.

Oddballs

The one that (he wished had) got away

This is the tale of a fisherman who probably would have wished his catch had been the one that got away.

On a fishing expedition in 1996, Franc Filipic caught a big one and was determined that this would be the one that would make his career. Unfortunately for the forty-seven-year-old from Ljubljana, Slovenia, he had caught a powerful specimen known as a sheatfish, similar to a catfish.

According to the state-run news agency, the fish pulled Franc under as he uttered his last words: 'Now I've got him!' His body was found after a two-day search.

The fish got away.

A devil of a deep blue sea

Not so much slip-ups as slippery customers befell the Volvo Ocean Race – a round-the-world event that began in Southampton in 2001.

It was reported in early 2002 that sailors were being

'attacked' by flying fish. The Australian sailor Anthony Nossiter was hit in the forehead by a fish measuring 25 centimetres.

Some of the Swedish competitors on the Rio-to-Miami leg were taking bets on who would be the first to catch one and eat it raw. It is not known whether anyone rose to the challenge, but no one seemed too keen.

Everyone's a winner, baby

In the figure skating competition at the 2002 Winter Olympics in Salt Lake City, huge controversy arose over a decision by a French judge to give her mark to the Russian pair, with the result that not one but two golds were awarded – one to the Russians and one to the Canadians.

The performance of the Russians, Yelena Berezhanaya and Anton Sikharulidze, was generally considered to be inferior to that of the Canadians, Jamie Sale and David Pelletier.

However, the French judge, Marie-Reine Le Gougne, seemed to disagree, and it was discovered that she had had pressure applied to favour the Russians. So there was uproar when it was clearly thought in all quarters that the Canadian pair should have been awarded the coveted prize.

An International Olympic Committee spokesperson said, 'The executive board has followed the International Skating Union proposal to award two gold medals and the votes of the French judge have been cancelled ...'

The IOC president Jacques Rogge said it was 'in the interests of the athletes'.

The scandal was dubbed, predictably, 'Skategate' by the tabloid media.

Slouch potatoes

Sport is supposed to make us all feel fitter and better, but as sports have become more accessible on the television, armchair spectators have begun to sustain injuries while viewing their favourite teams or players in action.

The most common injuries, it seems, are shoulder, neck and back sprains, which are caused when fans jump excitedly from their seats when their teams score. According to the Scottish tabloid, the *Daily Record*, even nil–nil draws can cause backache, as bored and sleepy fans slouch in their seats.

So the Chartered Society of Physiotherapists are recommending lumbar stretches, arm reaches, chest stretches and elbow flares to help to prevent injury. They also recommend that fans should wrap up warm, because cold muscles are more susceptible to injury.

The society's spokeswoman, Alison Fox, said: 'Injuries can be picked up just as easily watching the game at home.'

Well spotted!

In 1993 the Welsh national daily, the *Western Mail*, decided to make its 'Spot the Ball' competition just too easy.

With the accompanying slogan, 'It's so easy to be a winner', the paper had printed the previous week's solution instead of the current week's problem, complete with the arrow that helpfully pointed to the position of the ball, clearly visible against the sky.

Fortunately for the paper, the error was spotted after only a thousand papers had been run off.

Gold nearly went to pot

It was a close call for the Canadian snowboarder Ross Rebagliati, who won gold in the men's giant slalom at the 1998 Winter Olympics in Japan.

The drugs test showed a high level of marijuana in his bloodstream and he lost the gold. However, he maintained he had not smoked pot since April 1997. He blamed the high levels in his bloodstream to having inhaled other people's smoke at a going-away party. He was reinstated on a technicality and celebrated with a weekend in Amsterdam.

Homing away

The most mystifying pigeon race in history has to be the one in 1978, when 6,745 racing birds were released in Preston, Lancashire. Only 1,200 were ever seen again.

James Paterson, secretary of the Ayrshire Federation of Homing Pigeons, is quoted as saying, 'I've never known anything like it. They've vanished. Someone suggested they might have flown over a grouse moor and been shot. I can't believe they could have got all five thousand, five hundred and forty-five.'

The naturalist Tony Soper said that the missing birds had probably gone to the Devonshire seaside.

Tree cheers for Tom

Thomas Birch was not a very good fisherman. This eighteenth-century scholar hardly ever caught a fish, but so keen was he to do so that he decided on an unusual strategy.

He thought that his presence probably scared off all the fish, so he disguised himself as a tree. His arms fitted into the 'branches', and his eyes peered from knots in the 'bark'.

Off he went to the riverbank and stood there. And he stood. And he stood some more. All he managed to attract were a few birds, resting on his 'branches' and the occasional dog, which often made use of the base of his 'trunk'.

It's a gas!

At an ice hockey game between Olympia Heist and Griffoen Geel in Belgium in February 2002, players began to leave the ice, one by one, and so the disgruntled and confused audience responded with boos and shouts, believing the players to be giving in and giving up.

At the time of the first player's departure, Griffoen Geel were being beaten 6–3, which further fuelled the spectators' anger. Later in the game, however, fans began to leave too, feeling weak and ill.

After an investigation, it was discovered that the machine used for clearing the ice between matches had been pumping carbon monoxide out into the stadium.

A stadium spokesman told reporters, 'They were shouted at, because everybody thought the players couldn't accept they were losing.'

About 150 people in all needed hospital treatment: 112 managed to drive to the local hospital in Geel, while the others were taken by ambulance. It was left to the local fire brigade to check the stadium and eventually find the faulty machine.

Not so lucky gym!

Not all sporting slip-ups are committed by professionals, and not all by the sport's participants themselves.

There was a catalogue of disasters in 1998 when half a dozen Tottenham policewomen were among 200 people who went to Clacton-on-Sea in Essex to try to raise funds for a gymnastics club for north London youngsters. The astonishing story is to be found on the 'This Is Local London' website:

Things started to go wrong as the party gathered on Saturday morning at the beach to watch PC Debbie Michaels preparing for a sponsored parascend on a chute attached to a boat.

One of the bystanders, Alan Martin, got a part of the

parachute cord tangled around his neck and was hoisted 8 feet (2.5 metres) into the air when the boat began to move.

Witness and trip organizer Terry Goddard said: 'It was terrifying. He just managed to get free by pulling the cord loose and forcing the chute down.'

When PC Michaels did take off, the boat which was pulling her along sank after being deluged by a wave. She dropped into the water and had to be rescued by a lifeboat before the sinking vessel could drag her beneath the surface.

The boatman, Mr Goddard's brother Ricky, grabbed a lifejacket, jumped overboard and also needed saving by a craft of the Royal National Lifeboat Institution.

An attempt to salvage the £5,000 powerboat went wrong when group member Frank Bullock decided to try and drag it out using a 200ft rope attached to his brand new Range Rover on the beach.

Terry Goddard, 39, said: 'Frank's wheels got stuck in the sand and the tide began to come in. A passer-by offered to use a tractor to pull the car and boat out but that got stuck too and eventually the whole lot had to be freed by the Royal Navy.'

Earlier that afternoon Mark White, a trainer with the North London Paramount Gymnastics Club, broke his leg while giving a display on a trampoline at Clacton Pier.

Mr White was rushed to hospital in Colchester for surgery.

But strangest of all was the electrocution of a singer at an evening social function for the day-trippers at a working men's club in the town.

The singer of guitar band, Blind Beggar, was hurt when his microphone short-circuited, and someone who tried to help him also got a severe shock. Both were recovering this week.

Terry Goddard returned home on Monday to find his parked Ford Orion had been smashed into the boat, which had been brought up from Clacton on a tow truck.

And the final catastrophe was the discovery that his fridge-freezer had de-frosted, ruining £300 of food.

The jinxed weekend meant the organizers failed to raise the £1,500 needed to buy equipment for the gymnastics club, which is a registered charity.   (NORTH LONDON GUARDIAN NEWSPAPERS)

Not the pride of our Ally

When Scotland manager Ally MacLeod's national side were drawn against Iran in the 1978 World Cup, the odds were not on a win for the Scots.

Head in hands, MacLeod sat alone in the stadium, silently bemoaning his ill fortune, when a little dog gambolled up to him.

'Ah,' said MacLeod, 'my only wee friend in the entire world.' The dog did not agree, and bit him.

Recycled

Fifty-two-year-old Pedro Gatica was so keen to see the football World Cup that, in May 1986, he cycled from his home in Argentina to Mexico.

However, on arrival he found that he could not afford to get in. So he haggled for a ticket and, while he was doing so, thieves stole his bike.

Blast it!

A Canadian angler who was fishing in one of the country's many lakes was thrilled when he found that he had landed an enormous pike. He quickly dispatched it with a stick and laid it on the bank beside his shotgun.

However, the fish was not as dead as the angler thought and began to thrash about. Its tail caught on the trigger and ... It is not difficult to guess what happened next.

Whether the fish managed to thrash itself back into the water, it will never be known, but the luckless angler did not live to tell the tale.

Victory fit for a king

In 1973, Bobby Riggs displayed overt male chauvinist tendencies when he challenged Billie Jean King to a tennis match that would be a battle of the sexes.

Riggs had last been a Wimbledon champion in 1939, thirty-four years previously, but he was determined to beat this particular member of the sex that, he said, were at their prettiest when barefoot, pregnant, taking care of the children and working in the home.

'I want to set women's lib back twenty years, to get women back in the home where they belong,' he declared. 'I will scrape her up. She is a woman and is subject to women's emotional frailties. She will crack up during the match.'

And so the largest crowd in tennis history so far – about 39,000 – gathered to watch the match. King thrashed him 6–4, 6–3, 6–3.

Royal flush

Many people enjoy spotting royal spectators at Wimbledon, but how many have actually found one locked in the lavatory?

At one Wimbledon final, on hearing a distress call coming from the gents' toilets, Rosie Cherry shouldered open a locked door only to come face to face with a very relieved King George V.

Right royal defeat

In 1946 the Australian number-one seed for the men's Wimbledon singles title kept royalty waiting when he got lost on London Underground.

Dinny Pails was trying to get to the famous venue for his quarter-final clash with the French-born Indo-Chinese Yvon Petra. Having lost himself on the underground, Pails lost his game, so disconcerted was he by his experience, and the knowledge that Queen Mary was among the waiting spectators that day.

The late Mr Pigeon

The owner of the racing pigeon released in Pembrokeshire, West Wales, in June 1953 expected his prized bird to be home that evening, but he would never see it alive again.

Eleven years later, however, the bird did arrive home, but in a cardboard box, dead.

It had been sent all the way from Brazil.

Early bath

The Swedish skier Fredrik Nyberg had not even reached the piste before tearing ligaments in his knee. He fell into a stream on his way to a pre-race inspection in Kitzbühel, prematurely ending his skiing season.

Untimely

During the 1981 World Snooker Team Cup, the referee, John Smyth, decided he needed a new battery for his travelling alarm clock. He then pocketed the clock, complete with new battery, and forgot about it.

Then, while Smyth was refereeing a match between John Spencer and Paddy Morgan, the alarm clock sprung into life, causing play to be stopped while Smyth hurriedly located the off-switch.

Snapped – and out of it

At the 1956 Melbourne Olympics, it was a stray photographer that caused Britain's cyclists to settle for second place in the team time trial. Billy Holmes crashed into the photographer, who had wandered aimlessly on to the course, damaging his wheel.

Having to change the wheel meant the team lost valuable time, and ultimately they missed first place by just one second.

Weighty problem

A New Zealand bank clerk called Graham May had prepared well for his part in the super-heavyweight category of the weightlifting events at the 1974 Commonwealth Games.

The twenty-one-year-old was about to make a huge lift of 187.5 kilograms. However, as he jerked the bar over his head he suffered a minor blackout and fell from the stage to the floor of the hall.

The weight also fell, and having had some momentum, it careered across the floor, sending officials and spectators running for cover. May soon recovered and took gold.

Mets met with meteoric disaster

The New York Mets baseball team was formed in 1962. Before their first ever match they received a traditional American tickertape welcome down Broadway, with 40,000 spectators and a band.

When they did come to play, they had lost nine games in a row within a week, a run of losses matched only by the Brooklyn Dodgers in 1918. The Mets went on to lose more matches in one season than anyone else in the history of the game, with a final figure of 120 defeats.

Troubled waters

It was the occasion of the National Ambulance Service fishing championships at Kidderminster, Herefordshire, in 1972. But organizers had forgotten to inform the 200 expected participants of one vital fact.

On the appointed day, the anglers turned up and cast their lines. All day they sat, and not one of them got a bite. Eventually a passer-by informed them that they were wasting their time; the fish had all been moved to other waters three weeks before.

Hot and bothered

In a misguided effort to cool himself down during the 1950 Tour de France, cyclist Abd-el Kader Zaag drank a bottle of wine and promptly fell off his bike.

Having slept off his alcohol-induced torpor by the roadside, he climbed back into the saddle and sped off in the wrong direction.

A case of recycling?

After leading the classic mountain climb to Alpe d'Huez during the 1978 Tour de France, the Belgian rider Michel Pollentier was clearly worried by something that had found its way into his system, and so he decided to trick the drugs testers by using the urine of a team-mate.

The method of delivery was going to be a problem, though, as it had to look realistic when he produced his sample, so he decided to use a plastic pipe inside his shorts. Pollentier could have almost got away with the scam, but the size of the pipe drew unwanted attention to himself, raising considerable suspicion.

Ultimately he was not believed, and duly disqualified from the race.

Predator pussy pounced on pigeon Percy

Percy, the champion racing pigeon, slipped up badly when he forgot about the everyday dangers faced by ordinary birds.

After beating 1,000 rivals in a 500-mile race, powerful Percy flopped down exhausted in a Sheffield loft and was promptly eaten by a cat.

You're out

Bad news is usually delivered with care and sensitivity, but in the sporting world, managers and coaches can be brutal.

When the American baseball player Bob Uecker was dropped from a team, he said, 'They broke it to me gently. The manager came up to me before a game and told me they didn't allow visitors in the clubhouse.'

1066 and all that ...

A twenty-five-year-old man who lost his right eye in Portland, Oregon, in 1999, was lucky to be alive after an initiation into a men's rafting club went horribly wrong.

The club is called Mountain Men Anonymous, based in Grant's Pass, Oregon. The ceremony involved the shooting of a beer can from Tony Roberts's head with a hunting arrow.

Even the best shots can have an off-day. The arrow entered Roberts's right eye and, had it gone just a millimetre to the left, a major blood vessel would have been cut and he would have died instantly.

Dr Johnny Delashaw of the University Hospital in Portland said the arrow had gone through 20–25 centimetres (8–10 inches) of brain.

Roberts said afterwards, 'I feel so dumb about this.'

Buzz off!

The smallest of things can wreck the best-laid schemes, as events in the world billiards championship in September 1865 proved.

Louis Fox and John Deery were competing to win $40,000 in the ballroom of the Washington Hotel, and Fox quickly went into the lead.

Ball after ball plopped into the pockets, but suddenly a fly that had been merrily buzzing its way around the room for much of the day landed on the cue ball.

Fox shooed it away, but it came back, and back again. So this time he waved his cue to shoo it away, but hit the cue ball. This was technically a foul shot, and he forfeited his chance to continue that break.

So back into the game came Deery, who eventually won the match.

A load of bull

In Betulia, Colombia, in 1999, the town's annual carnival took place, including five days of amateur bullfighting. No bull was killed, but dozens of would-be matadors were badly hurt.

One participant said, 'It's just one bull against a town of a thousand morons.'

Freddie's foxy footwork

One of the most unusual sports must be the British Mascot Grand National at Huntingdon racecourse. There was controversy when Freddie the Fox (representing the Countryside Appreciation Group) crossed the finishing line first, and a grovelling apology had to be made.

It all began when doubts were expressed over Freddie's footwear, as he seemed to be wearing spiked training shoes. Eventually, the speedy mascot was unmasked, and revealed to be Matthew Douglas, an Olympic 400-metres hurdler, and a semi-finalist in the 2000 Olympic Games in Sydney.

There were even more doubts about whether the

organization he claimed to represent really existed.

An inquiry was launched to decide whether Freddie was a legitimate contestant if he was a professional athlete. Huddled conversations took place as rules were scoured, and it was eventually decided to give the victory to Dazzler the Lion, representing Rushden and Diamonds. The second place went to Oldham Athletic's Chaddy the Owl.

The racecourse manager, Jim Allen, announced that Freddie's owners were happy to concede: 'They have accepted that in the spirit of the race they should not have done what they did. They did it for a laugh; they did it for a bit of fun and they didn't realize the interest that this race attracts … they've held their hands up and said, "Sorry, we shouldn't have done it. We want you to disqualify us."'

Out of the Mouths
of Sportsmen and
Commentators ...

Some of the most memorable sporting slip-ups are those of the spoken variety; a range of astounding blunders from the mouths of sportsmen and sports commentators across the globe.

The following quotes were either uttered on television, spoken on radio, printed in newspapers or posted on websites.

There is always one personality who puts his foot in his mouth more than others. With commentators, it was David Coleman; with football managers, Kevin Keegan. Here is a selection of some of their best efforts.

'Chile have three options – they could win or they could lose.'

'England can end the millennium as it started – as the greatest football nation in the world.'

'Bobby Robson must be thinking of throwing some fresh legs on.'

'England have the best fans in the world and Scotland's fans are second to none.'

'He's using his strength and that is his strength – his strength.'

'They compare Steve McManaman to Steve Heighway and he's nothing like him, but I can see why – it's because he's a bit different.'

'I came to Nantes two years ago, and it's much the same today, except that it's totally different.'

'Gary always weighed up his options, especially when he had no choice.'

'I don't think there's anyone bigger or smaller than Maradona.'

'I know what is around the corner – I just don't know where the corner is. But the onus is on us to perform and we must control the bandwagon.'

'I'd love to be a mole on the wall in the Liverpool dressing room at half-time.'

'In some ways, cramp is worse than having a broken leg.'

'It's like a toaster, the ref's shirt pocket – every time there's a tackle, up pops a yellow card.'

'It's understandable that people are keeping one eye on the pot and another up the chimney.'

'The thirty-three- or thirty-four-year-olds will be thirty-six or thirty-seven by the time the next World Cup comes around, if they're not careful.'

'The tide is very much in our court now.'

And the rest ...

Vinnie Jones once explained why he chose not to apply for the Queen's Park Rangers manager's job with the words, 'I've plenty of bows to my string.'

For the Welsh soccer star Ryan Giggs, one wing is as good as another: 'It was just like playing on the left. Except it was on the right,' he quipped.

Wimbledon's Michael Hughes gave us the benefit of his anatomical knowledge when he said, 'The groin's been a little sore but I've put it to the back of my head.'

The US Olympic basketball coach Bobby Knight was not too fond of the professional version of his chosen sport: 'I don't even watch pro basketball. If I had the choice of watching a pro basketball game or two mice making it on television, I'd watch the mice. Even if the screen was fuzzy.'

When Jimmy Hill was practising saying the name Nigel Starmer-Smith in preparation for an interview with the rugby player, he repeated the name over and over again. At the time of the live interview, however, Hill got the name right, but then said that Starmer-Smith 'had seven craps as scum half for England'.

The Derby boss Jim Smith must have forgotten the concept of time when he said, 'At the moment, we're not interested in the Cup: we're only interested in the present day – and that's Charlton tomorrow.'

Struggling with his arithmetic, David Coleman declared, 'And here's Moses Kiptanui – the nineteen-year-old Kenyan who turned twenty a few weeks ago.'

Harry Carpenter was commentating on the 'Rumble in the Jungle' boxing match in 1974 in Zaïre (now the Democratic Republic of the Congo). Muhammad Ali and George Foreman were slugging it out, when Carpenter said, 'That's it. There's no way Ali can win this one now.' At which point Ali knocked Foreman out.

The American tennis ace John McEnroe was well known for his colourful turn of phrase. After being fined in the US Open for calling the umpire a 'fat turd', he said, 'If I'd known I was going to be fined for that, I'd really have let him have it.'

Murray Walker, the famous motor-racing commentator, is equally feted for his verbal gaffes. When fully absorbed in the action taking place on a motor-racing circuit, adrenaline is pumping and there is little time to think before one speaks, and sometimes one's commentary makes little or no sense whatsoever:

'Well let's, uh, lugsh— luxurrriate in a little hypothesis and try to work out what, if anything, is wrong with Alain Prost. [Prost was being caught by Berger late in the race.] Has he got tyre problems? Very unlikely. Is Prost having fuel trouble? Well, who knows? I think it's a bit unlikely. Is Prost having gearbox trouble? I can't tell you. And, since P—, uh, Prost is unlikely to come on the radio and let me know, you'll have to guess along with me.'

Doubtless the former England football manager Howard Wilkinson did not intend to be indelicate when he said, 'Once Tony Daley opens his legs you've got a problem.'

Ken Norton, dejected after a defeat by Muhammad Ali in 1976, was consoled by Harry Carpenter with the comforting words, 'If you hadn't been there it wouldn't have been much of a fight.'

David Coleman probably knew what he meant when he said, 'It's a great advantage to be able to hurdle with both legs.'

During Tiger Woods' rookie year on the golfing circuit, Sandy Lyle was asked what he thought of the up and coming young Woods: 'I don't know. I've never played there.'

Joe Namath of the New York Jets, the US football side, was asked whether he preferred Astroturf to grass. 'I don't know,' replied Joe. 'I've never smoked Astroturf.'

Was the motor-racing commentator Murray Walker being mischievous when he uttered the classic, 'We now have exactly the same situation as we had at the start of the race, only exactly the opposite'?

The Newcastle soccer manager Bobby Robson got it just about right after his team had played Cameroon in the 1990 World Cup: 'We didn't underestimate them. They were just a lot better than we thought.'

Dan Osinski, the US baseball player, was asked by a waitress whether he wanted his pizza cut into six pieces or eight. 'Better make it six,' he said. 'I can't eat eight.'

Speaking of the difficulties of adjusting to playing football and living in Italy, Ian Rush commented, 'It was like being in a foreign country.'

Equivocal to the last, the former England soccer team coach Terry Venables sounded certain of his somewhat vague judgment when he was asked by Jimmy Hill, 'Don't sit on the fence, Terry. What chance do you think Germany has of getting through?' Venables replied, 'I think it's fifty–fifty.'

Unintentional double entendres are rife in the sporting world, especially in games involving spherical objects or requiring certain positions to be adopted. Snooker commentator Ted Lowe proved this to be the case with, 'Fred Davis, the doyen of snooker, now sixty-seven years of age and too old to get his leg over, prefers to use his left hand.'

There is nothing like precision. The boxing promoter Don King, when introducing the victorious boxer Asumah Nelson, said, 'Here's the man of the hour at this particular moment.'

Benito Mussolini never minced words. A telegram from him to the 1938 Italian World Cup final team had the message, 'Win or die'.

During a commentary with Bernie Ecclestone of Formula One fame, Murray Walker asked him, 'In the seventeen years since you bought McLaren, which of your many achievements do you think was the most memorable?' Bernie responded with, 'Well I don't remember buying McLaren.' (Bernie Ecclestone used to own the Brabham team.)

Determined to succeed at all costs, Rod Brookin, a former basketball player for the University of Pittsburgh claimed, 'I'm going to graduate on time, no matter how long it takes.'

The former Manchester United manager Ron Atkinson has principles, it seems, if this 1979 quote is anything to go by: 'I never comment on referees and I'm not going to break the habit of a lifetime for that prat.'

Frank Bruno was never short of a quip at the height of his career: 'I was in a no-win situation, so I'm glad that I won rather than lost.'

David Coleman was stating the obvious when he said, 'There's going to be a real ding-dong when the bell goes.' And he knew what it meant to be alone in a crowd with the remark, 'There is Brendan Foster, by himself, with twenty thousand people.'

Steve Webber, the University of Georgia baseball coach was probably unaware he was stating the obvious when, after a game in the Louisiana Superdome, he said, 'It was a little different. It was like playing inside.'

When the San Francisco Giants' play-by-play man, Hank Greenwald, was asked to shorten his pre-game talk at the Tree Rivers Stadium, no one expected him to reduce his introduction to: 'Hello, everybody, and welcome to Two Rivers Stadium'.

Murray Walker's eyes were clearly not deceiving him – or were they? 'And here comes Damon Hill in the Williams. This car is absolutely unique – except for the one behind it, which is exactly the same.'

The boxing promoter Don King was capable of modesty, it seems: 'I never cease to amaze myself. I say that humbly.' And on another occasion: 'I am the best promoter in the world. And I say that humbly.'

The Nottingham Forest and England soccer star Stuart Pearce must have seen the light when he said in 1992, 'I can see the carrot at the end of the tunnel.'

How many parents did Greg Norman have in mind when he said, 'I owe a lot to my parents, especially my mother and father'?

The golfer Davis Love III was not enamoured of newspaper cameramen, it seems, after his swing was affected by a flash: 'What's the penalty for killing a photographer – one stroke or two?'

Murray Walker's brain was obviously racing at Formula 1 pace when he observed, 'Just under ten seconds for Nigel Mansell. Call it nine point five seconds in round numbers.'

Perhaps geography was never Ron Greenwood's strong point: 'Playing with wingers is more effective against European sides like Brazil than English sides like Wales.'

Nor was knowledge of the human body for Joe Sheldon: 'A brain scan revealed that Andrew Caddick is not suffering from stress fracture of the shin.'

Judging distance is not everyone's strong point, either: 'That's inches away from being millimetre perfect,' said the snooker commentator Ted Lowe.

It was a case of 'Beware the ides of March', when the former Hull, Manchester and England player Stuart Pearson said, 'Bobby Gould thinks I'm trying to stab him in the back. In fact I'm right behind him.'

If Terry Venables had put a bet on this prediction, he would probably have won: 'If history repeats itself, I should think we can expect the same thing again.'

When commentating on the annual Oxford-Cambridge University boat race, John Snagge did his best to clear up any confusion regarding the race leaders: 'It's a desperately close race. I can't quite tell who's ahead – it's either Oxford or Cambridge.'

Following those who are arithmetically challenged and those who are geographically challenged, enter Tony Cozier, the geometrically challenged: 'The Queen's Park Oval, exactly as its name suggests – absolutely round.'

Chris Turner, the Peterborough manager, really knew how to make a player feel wanted when, before a League Cup quarter-final in 1992, he said, 'I've told the players we need to win so that I can have the cash to buy some new ones.'

Money was clearly burning a hole in George Best's pocket at the height of his career: 'I spent a lot of my money on booze, birds and fast cars. The rest I just squandered.'

Not so much a slip-up, this, but certainly an astute and amusing piece of management from John Lambie, the manager of Partick Thistle, when he was told that a concussed striker didn't know who he was: 'That's great. Tell him he's Pelé and get him back on.'

Football managers' lives are so busy that you can excuse them if they forget where they are occasionally. Take this from the former England soccer team coach Terry Venables, who told Capital Gold, 'If you can't stand the heat in the dressing room, get out of the kitchen.'

We dearly wish we knew who said this, quoted on a humour website, but all we know is that it was on Radio 5 Live: 'It's now one-all, an exact reversal of the score on Saturday.'

The anatomically challenged again – this time the radio presenter Tom Ferrie: 'Dumbarton player Steve McCahill has limped off with a badly cut forehead.'

There's winning and there's winning. This team could have been in no doubt when the legendary commentator Brian Moore, said, 'Newcastle, of course, unbeaten in their last five wins ...'

The cricket commentator David Acfield was obviously mesmerized by the grace that slow motion brings to the instant replay when he observed, most astutely, 'Strangely, in slow-motion replay, the ball seemed to hang in the air for even longer.'

One wonders what the former Tottenham Hotspur and Bristol Rovers manager Gerry Francis did say to his players, even if he was getting his media in a twist: 'What I said to them at half-time would be unprintable on the radio.'

Oscar Wilde once observed that the British and the Americans are separated by a common language. Remembering first that Americans have a preference for skipping the preposition (on) before a day of the week, note the comma in this New York Post headline from 1993: 'John Harkes going to Sheffield, Wednesday.'

Mick Lyons – footballer turned philosopher: 'If there weren't such a thing as football, we'd all be frustrated footballers.'

Less anatomically challenged is Derek Johnstone who, in 1994, said on BBC TV Scotland: 'He's one of those footballers whose brains are in his head.'

Even the consummate professionals like Barry Davies lose their way occasionally: 'The crowd think that Todd handled the ball ... they must have seen something that nobody else did.'

Sometimes you have to clutch at straws – and obvious statements – when called upon to defend a meagre playing record, as the Italian soccer coach Arrigo Sacchi did with, 'You don't have to have been a horse to be a jockey.'

Wimbledon's Dean Holdsworth was not too enamoured of the club's football prowess when he quipped, 'The only way we will be going to Europe is if the club splash out and take us all to Eurodisney.'

Ron Atkinson is another character with a talent for the spoken sporting slip-up:

'They've picked their heads up off the ground and they now have a lot to carry on their shoulders.'

'He's almost hit that too well.'

'He sliced the ball when he had it on a plate.'

'Zidane is not very happy, because he's suffering from the wind.'

'Well, either side could win it, or it could be a draw.'

'I'm afraid they've left their legs at home.'

'Beckenbauer really has gambled all his eggs.'

'I think that was a moment of cool panic there.'

'I'm going to make a prediction – it could go either way.'

'He dribbles a lot and the opposition don't like it – you can see it all over their faces.'

'I would not say he [David Ginola] is the best left-winger in the Premiership, but there are none better.'

Ron Atkinson must have thought well of Gordon Strachan, aged thirty-nine, when he made this comparison: 'There's nobody fitter at his age, except maybe Raquel Welch.'

Stuart Hall of Radio 5 Live was obviously distracted when he asked, 'What will you do when you leave football, Jack? Will you stay in football?'

Speaking on Sky Sports, Dave Bassett was probably looking through fogged glasses and saw three posts when he said, 'An inch or two either side of the post and that would have been a goal.'

Nothing like stating the obvious, as the footballer Peter Withe did, speaking on Radio 5 Live: 'Both sides have scored a couple of goals, and both sides have conceded a couple of goals.'

Another from Radio 5 Live saw Alan Green with an assessment of what makes a good goal scorer: 'You don't score sixty-four goals in eighty-six games at the highest level without being able to score goals.'

Alex Ferguson had probably not kitted his lads out with boots for this match: 'The lads really ran their socks into the ground.'

'And I suppose they [Spurs] are nearer to being out of the FA Cup now than any other time since the first half of this season, when they weren't ever in it anyway' – John Motson, BBC.

Another gem from the anatomically challenged from John Greig: 'Celtic manager Davie Hay still has a fresh pair of legs up his sleeve.'

Pity Ron Greenwood's squad if they were as self-punishing as he implied when observing, 'They have missed so many chances they must be wringing their heads in shame.'

Another case of stating the obvious, this time from the footballer Derek Rae: 'It's headed away by John Clark, using his head.'

If you have two names you are two entities, according to the commentator Mike Ingham: 'Tottenham are trying tonight to become the first London team to win this cup. The last team to do so was the 1973 Spurs side.'

Was John Motson letting his bias show when he observed, 'The game is balanced in Arsenal's favour'?

Radio 5 Live's Alan Green certainly knew how to mix his transport metaphors: 'It was that game that put the Everton ship back on the road.'

Richard Park must have caught the bug: 'Celtic were at one time nine points ahead, but somewhere along the road, their ship went off the rails.'

In 1945 the women's golfing magazine, *Fairway & Hazard*, was previewing the Curtis Cup, and wanted to convey a message to the British team captain, Baba Beck. The message should have read, 'And so, Mrs Beck, Good Luck and bring back to Britain that coveted Trophy.'

Unfortunately, a printing gremlin had got into the works, and what appeared was, 'And sod Mrs Beck ...

And finally ...

Rounding off this section of verbal sporting slip-ups are a few quick-fire quotes without comment; after all, most of them speak for themselves ...

'In terms of the Richter Scale, this defeat was a force-eight gale'
– John Lyall

'History is all about todays and not about yesterdays'
– Brian Moore

'In comparison, there's no comparison' *– Ron Greenwood*

'I never make predictions and I never will' *– Paul Gascoigne*

'Mirandinha will have more shots this afternoon than both sides put together' *– Malcolm McDonald*

'Being naturally right-footed, he doesn't often chance his arm with his left foot' *– Trevor Brooking*

'Glenn Hoddle hasn't been the Hoddle we know. Neither has Bryan Robson' *– Ron Greenwood*

'If we played like that every week we wouldn't be so inconsistent' *– Bryan Robson*

'There's no way Ryan Giggs is another George Best. He's another Ryan Giggs' *– Denis Law*

'You guys line up alphabetically by height'
– Bill Peterson, Florida state football coach

'... and he crosses the line with the ball almost mesmerically tied to his foot with a ball of string' – *Ian Darke, Radio 5 Live*

'For those of you watching in black and white, Spurs are in the all-yellow strip' – *John Motson, BBC*

'Barcelona ... a club with a stadium that seats a hundred and twenty thousand people. And they're all here in Newcastle tonight!' – *Brian Moore*

'Ronaldo is always very close to being either onside or offside' – *Ray Wilkins, Metro Radio commentator*

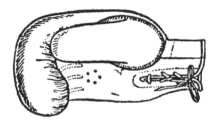

'You can sum up this sport in two words: you never know'
– *the American boxing trainer Lou Duva*

'If England are going to win this match, they're going to have to score a goal' – *Jimmy Hill*

'You weigh up the pros and cons and try to put them into chronological order' – *Dave Bassett*

'Robert Lee was able to do some running on his groin for the first time' – *Glenn Hoddle*

'I was saying the other day, how often the most vulnerable area for goalies is between their legs' – *Andy Gray, Sky Sports*

'The lad got overexcited when he saw the whites of the goalposts' eyes' – *Steve Coppell, Radio 5 Live*

'And Nakano tries to avoid being passed by his team-mate Trulli, which should in fact be quite easy, because Trulli is going more slowly than his team-mate Nakano' – *Murray Walker*

'They [Rosenborg] have won sixty-six games, and they've scored in all of them' – *Brian Moore, ITV*

'That's twice now he [Terry Phelan] has got between himself and the goal' – *Brian Marwood, Radio 5 Live*

'We threw our dice into the ring and turned up trumps' – *Bruce Rioch*

'And there's Ray Clemence looking as cool as ever out in the cold' – *Jimmy Hill*

'You give one hundred per cent in the first half of the game, and, if that's not enough, in the second half you give what's left' – *Yogi Berra*

'If the gloves weren't off before, and they were, they sure are now!' – *Murray Walker*

'And Arsenal now have plenty of time to dictate the last few seconds' – *Peter Jones*

'The only thing I have in common with George Best is that we come from the same place, play for the same club and were discovered by the same man' – *Norman Whiteside*

'Nobody goes to that restaurant any more. It's too crowded' – *Yogi Berra*

'You might not think that's cricket, and it's not: it's motor racing' – *Murray Walker*

'So, this movie you star in, *The Life Story of George Best* – tell us what it's about' – *George Gavin, Sky Sport*

'And we all know that in football if you stand still you go backwards' – *Peter Reid, Tyne Tees television*

'Street hockey is great for kids. It's energetic, competitive, and skilful. And best of all it keeps them off the street' – *Radio 1 Newsbeat*

'It was the fastest-ever swim over that distance on American soil' – *Greg Phillips, Portsmouth News*

'A fascinating duel between three men ...' – *David Coleman*

'I'm glad two sides of the cherry have been put forward' – *Geoff Boycott*

'There are the boys, their balls between their legs' – *Amanda Redington, GMTV*

'Ian Mackie is here to prove his back injury is behind him' – *commentator at Spar Athletics*

'Azinger is wearing an all-black outfit: black jumper, blue trousers, white shoes and a pink "tea-cosy" hat'
– Renton Laidlaw

'The advantage of the rain is, that if you have a quick bike, there's no advantage' *– Barry Sheene*

'I wouldn't be surprised if this game went all the way to the finish' *– Ian St John*

'Apart from their goals, Norway haven't scored'
– Terry Venables

'The Croatians don't play well without the ball' *– Barry Venison*

'People always said I shouldn't be burning my candle at both ends. Maybe that's because they don't have a big enough candle' *– George Best*

'Viv Anderson has pissed a fatness test' *– John Helm, commentator*

'The swimmers are swimming out of their socks'
– Sharron Davies, BBC

'In cycling, you can put all your money on one horse'
– Stephen Roche, Eurosport

'A goalkeeper is a goalkeeper because he can't play football'
– Ruud Gullit

'I left because of illness and fatigue. The fans were sick and tired of me' *– John Ralston, former coach with the Denver Broncos*

'I always used to put my right boot on first, and then obviously my right sock' *– Barry Venison, ITV*

'The spirit at this club [Sheffield United] is the worst I've ever known, and the tea's not much better, either' – *Dave Bassett*

'Without being too harsh on David, he cost us the match' – *Ian Wright, ITV*

'It's a very well-run outfit from Monday to Friday. It's Saturdays we've got a problem with' – *Lawrie McMenemy, on Southampton*

'It's amazing how, in this part of the world, history has been part of its past' – *David Duffy, Eurosport*

'I'm a great fan of baseball. I watch a lot of games on the radio' – *Gerald Ford, former US president*

'Football's not a matter of life and death. It's much more important than that' – *Bill Shankly*

'They [Leeds] used to be a bit like Arsenal, winning by one goal to nil, or even less' – *Nasser Hussain, Channel 5*

'It took me seventeen years to get three thousand hits in baseball. I did it in one afternoon on the golf course' – *Hank Aaron, baseball player*

'I was eighteen about six years ago. I'm twenty-eight now' – *Frank Bruno*

'Football hooligans? Well, there are ninety-two club chairmen for a start' – *Brian Clough*

'The pace of the match is really accelerating, by which I mean it's getting faster all the time' – *David Coleman*

'The first thing that went wrong was half-time. We could have done without that' – *Graham Taylor*

'Billiards is very similar to snooker, except there are only three balls and no one watches it' – *Steve Davis*

'Poland nil, England nil – though England are now looking better value for their nil' – *Barry Davies*

'Batistuta gets most of his goals with the ball' – *Ian St John*

'Do my eyes deceive me or is Senna's car sounding a bit rough?' – *Murray Walker*

'My golf game's gone off so much that when I went fishing recently my first cast missed the lake' – *Ben Crenshaw*

'He [Brian Laudrup] wasn't just facing one defender: he was facing one at the front and one at the back as well' – *Trevor Steven, STV*

'The sound of the ball hitting the batsman's skull was music to my ears' – *Jeff Thomson*

'We definitely will be improved this year. Last year we lost ten games. This year we only scheduled nine'
– *Ray Jenkins, Montana state football team coach*

'Football today, it's like a game of chess: it's all about money'
– *Newcastle United fan, Radio 5 Live*

'Ah! Isn't that nice? The wife of the Cambridge president is kissing the cox of the Oxford crew'
– *Harry Carpenter, 1977 Boat Race*

'Footballers are no different from human beings'
– *Graham Taylor*

'I'm not a believer in luck, although I do believe you need it'
– *Alan Ball*

'He's accused of being arrogant, unable to cope with the press and a boozer. Sounds like he's got a chance to me'
– *George Best on Paul Gascoigne, 1988*

'I wouldn't ever set out to hurt anybody deliberately, unless it was, you know, important – like a league game or something'
– *Dick Buktus, Chicago Bears*

'I've got five back-up systems. The fifth one's called the Lord's Prayer' – *Evel Knievel*

The World Cup – truly an international event' – *John Motson*

'If it moves, you kick it. If it doesn't move, you kick it till it does'
– *Phil Woosnam, a former Welsh international, teaching football to Americans*

'I've got a gut feeling in my stomach' – *Alan Sugar, BBC1*

'The new West Stand casts a giant shadow over the entire pitch, even on a sunny day' – *Chris Ones in the* Evening Standard

'Unfortunately, we keep kicking ourselves in the foot'
– *Ray Wilkins, BBC1*